THE
BIG PHONICS
BOOK

GRADES 1-3

AUTHORS
BARBARA GREGORICH
JEAN SYSWERDA
ARLENE HENKEL

CONSULTANT
LORIE DE YOUNG

ILLUSTRATORS
CHRIS COOK
JOE BODDY

The Big Phonics Book is a compilation of favorite titles from the **I Know It!** series. The ten titles are listed in the table of contents.

CONTENTS

An answer key is provided at the end of each skill area.

PARENT GUIDE

The skills in **The Big Phonics Book** are those most commonly taught at the first through third grade levels. Here are some suggestions for working with your child at home:

- Don't do too many pages at one sitting. The size of the book could overwhelm the child. Remove a few pages at a time. (Pages are perforated for easy removal.) Praise each completed page. Page by page, day to day, is the best.

- If your child is puzzled by one activity, move on to another. The activities are ordered, but there's nothing magical about that order.

- Do the activities at a particular time of day, perhaps before snack time. Do them when the child is not tired. Discuss the learning experience. Be enthusiastic: "Let's work in our school books today! Do you remember what you did yesterday?"

- Enjoy it! Laugh a lot! Discuss the activity. Most activities can be done independently by the child, since directions are clear and consistent. Never use an activity as punishment. Don't expect too much. The activities are meant as practice.

- There will be days when your child may not feel like working. This is typical, so accept it. And remember: The communication patterns you establish today will pay off as your child grows older.

LONG A SOUND: ai

The Great Longo is a magician! He makes long vowel words! Sometimes he makes words with a long <u>a</u> sound. He makes them by putting <u>ai</u> together! What magic!

Help the Great Longo. He wants you to add long <u>a</u> words to his magic chain. Look at each picture. Say the picture word. Write the letters <u>ai</u> on the blank lines. Say the word. Then write the words on Great Longo's magic chain.

t r ___ ___ n

s n ___ ___ l

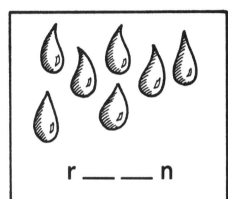

r ___ ___ n

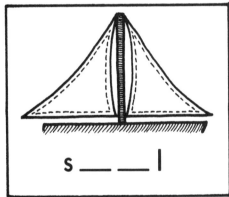

s ___ ___ l

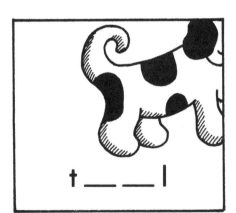

t ___ ___ l

p ___ ___ l

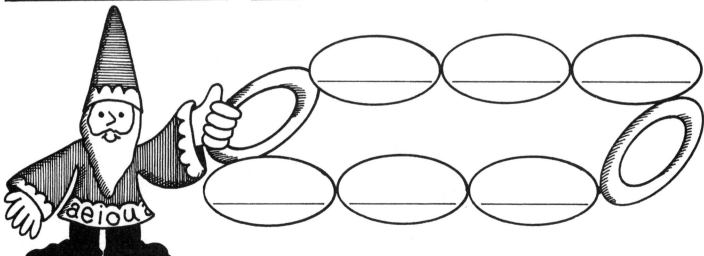

3

LONG A SOUND: ay

Make a long a playhouse! Make it with ay bricks! Look at the pictures at the bottom of the page. Say the picture word. Then write ay on the line to finish the word. The letters ay help make a long a sound! Write a long a word on each brick of the playhouse.

h ___ ___

s p r ___ ___

p r ___ ___ ___

c r ___ ___ o n

t r ___ ___

j ___ ___

M ___ ___

What say we just play all day?

LONG A SOUND: eigh

Once the Great Longo had a long <u>a</u> party. He called it the <u>eigh</u> party. Fill in the blanks to find out what happened. Use the <u>eigh</u> words at the bottom of the page to help you.

1. First, Longo had __ __ __ __ __ big cakes.

2. Then he started to __ __ __ __ __ himself.

3. "Oh, no!" he said. "My __ __ __ __ __ __ is over 200 pounds!"

4. "I'll be as big as a __ __ __ __ __ __ __ train," he added.

5. "I've got to stop. I won't eat for __ __ __ __ __ days!"

eight	weight	weigh
freight	eight	

5

LONG A SOUND: silent e

The Great Longo has a magic wand! It is called the silent e wand!
The silent e wand changes words. You can help the Great Longo
change words. Look at the pictures. Say the first picture word.
See how it is spelled. Say the second picture word. Write the
letters of the first word on the lines. Then add an e. Say the new
word. Do you hear what the magic e wand can do?

m a n   _ _ _ _

c a n   _ _ _ _

p a n   _ _ _ _

c a p   _ _ _ _

LONG A SOUND: silent e

The Great Longo is still using his silent e wand! He is making long a words out of other words by adding a silent e! Read each sentence. Write in the blank the silent e word that begins like the underlined word. Say the silent e word. Hear the long a sound!

| pale | hate | pane | plane | cane |

1. I _____ to wear this <u>hat</u>.

2. He threw the <u>pan</u> through the window _____.

3. You <u>can</u> walk with a _____.

4. My <u>pal</u> looked sick and _____.

5. I <u>plan</u> to fly on a _____.

LONG A SOUND REVIEW

Color each long _a_ word blue. Then see what you find!

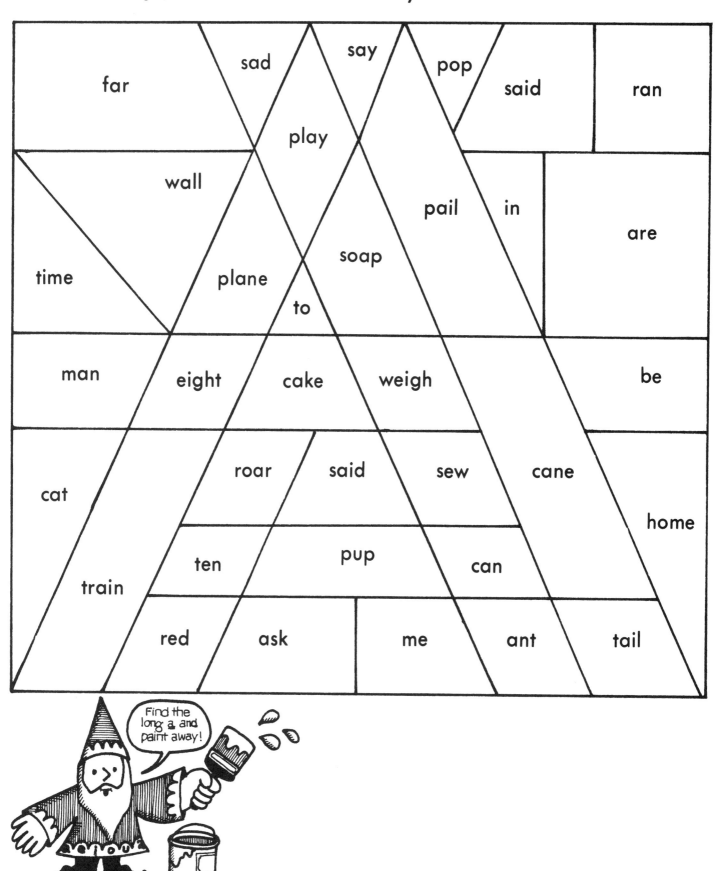

far · sad · say · pop · said · ran · play · wall · pail · in · are · time · soap · plane · to · man · eight · cake · weigh · be · cat · roar · said · sew · cane · home · ten · pup · can · train · red · ask · me · ant · tail

Find the long _a_ and paint away!

8

LONG A SOUND: REVIEW

The Great Longo is driving a long a train. He wants to fill the train cars with long a words. Look at the list at the bottom of the page. Then write only the long a words on the cars of the train.

stay	ran	rain	made	take	mad
hat	car	day	bake	pail	gray

LONG E SOUND: ee

Help the Great Longo trap the buzzing bee! Help the Great Longo block all the doors with long e words. The long e words are made by the letters ee together. Look at each picture. Then write the correct word by the picture.

| sheep | three | wheel | teeth | teepee | tree |

LONG E SOUND: ea

Sometimes the letters ea make the long e sound. Look at each picture. Say the name of the picture. Write ea in the blanks. Then write the word below the picture. Say the word.

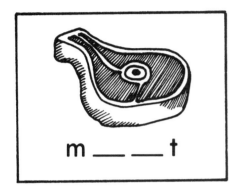

m __ __ t

_____

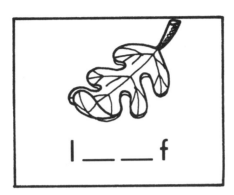

l __ __ f

_____

s __ __ l

_____

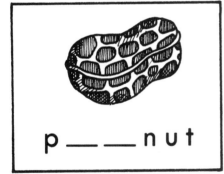

p __ __ n u t

_____

__ __ g l e

_____

w h __ __ t

_____

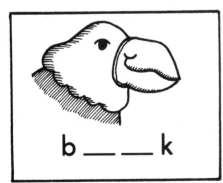

b __ __ k

_____

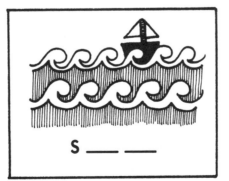

s __ __

_____

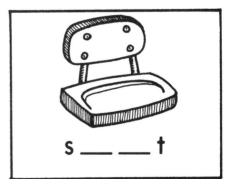

s __ __ t

_____

LONG E SOUND: ey

The Great Longo makes magic with the letters ey. They make the long e sound at the end of some words. Look at each picture. Draw a line from the picture to the word. Write the word.

key

_____

monkey

_____

donkey

_____

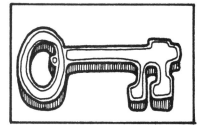

hockey

_____

money

_____

turkey

_____

Don't ask me why, but it works!

12

LONG E SOUND: ie, e

Help the Great Longo catch a thief! Look at each picture.
Then write the correct word by the picture. Say the word.
Hear the long e sound.

field   chief   cookie   thief   priest   he   she

13

LONG E SOUND REVIEW

The Great Longo is hiding things! He is hiding things that are spelled with a long e sound! Look at the words at the bottom of the page. Then look at the picture. Find the things that have a long e sound. Circle them.

bee	tree	cookie	turkey	penny
key	leaf	peanut	wheel	teepee

14

LONG E SOUND REVIEW

Look at each picture. Say the word. Circle <u>Yes</u> if the word has a long <u>e</u> sound. Circle <u>No</u> if it does not.

thief

Yes   No

sheep

Yes   No

bed

Yes   No

peach

Yes   No

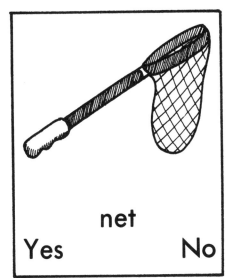

net

Yes   No

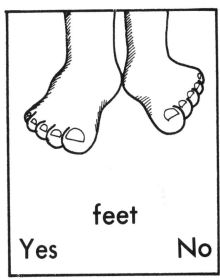

feet

Yes   No

men

Yes   No

bee

Yes   No

monkey

Yes   No

LONG I SOUND: ie, y

The Great Longo makes the long i sound in words. He does it by using the letter y or the letters ie! The Great Longo is tricky!

Look at each picture. Then fill in the blanks next to each picture with two words that rhyme. Use the words at the bottom of the page.

	Birds _____ in the _____.
	A _____ must be very _____.
	_____ sister is very _____.
	Some animals _____ down and seem to _____.
	Some _____ fell on my _____.
	_____ not to _____.

fly	pie	spy	my	try	lie
die	sky	cry	shy	tie	sly

16

LONG I SOUND: igh

The Great Longo is being chased by Mighty Moose! Help the Great Longo get away. Write the correct word by the picture.

knight   night   light   thigh   high   fight   fright

LONG I SOUND: ild, ind

The Great Longo is making riddles. The answers are long i
words that end in ild or ind. Read each riddle. Then write in the
blank the correct long i word from the list at the bottom of the page.

1. A horse that is not tame is _____.

2. A little person is a _____.

3. I think with my _____.

4. If you can't see, you are _____.

5. If you lose something, someone may _____ it.

6. If you help people, you are _____.

blind	wild	child	mind	find	kind

LONG I SOUND: silent e

The Great Longo is making silent e words again! This time his words all have the long i sound. Look at the pictures. Write the i in the blank space inside each word. Then draw a line from each word to the right picture.

d __ m e

t __ m e

b __ k e

k __ t e

w r __ t e

t __ r e

f __ r e

p __ p e

These words will be mine, if you draw the right line!

19

LONG I SOUND: REVIEW

The Great Longo is on a long i butterfly chase! Help him by coloring each butterfly that has a long i word written on it. Try to catch all the long i butterflies!

20

LONG I SOUND: REVIEW

Read each word and say each picture word. Put a circle around the word or picture in each row that has a long i sound.

i	(fly)	(pig)	(dog)
i	give	pie	whip
i	(bone)	(bed)	(bicycle)
i	gift	tire	dig
i	(pipe)	(tree)	(flower)
i	baby	bee	dime
i	(iron)	(ring)	(six)
i	five	eight	six

LONG O SOUND: oe, oa

The Great Longo makes long o words in many tricky ways.
Sometimes he uses oe to make the long o sound. Sometimes he uses
oa to make the long o sound!

Look at each picture. Write in the missing letters. Say the word. Then
write all the long o words on the Great Longo's boat.

t _ _

h _ _

d _ _

r _ _ d

c _ _ t

t _ _ st

b _ _ t

g _ _ t

t _ _ d

Let's load up and float away!

LONG O SOUND: o, ow, old, ost

The Great Longo is making long o riddles! He makes the long o sound with o, ow, old, or ost! How tricky! Read the riddle. Then write in the correct answer.

If you know, just say so!

1. Get ready, get set, _____!

2. I eat my soup from a _____.

3. White _____ fell from the sky.

4. _____is bright and shiny.

5. Did you see a _____ on Halloween?

6. The black bird in the tree was a _____.

7. If it's not yes, it is _____.

8. If you are not young, you are _____.

bowl	old	no	gold
go	ghost	crow	snow

LONG O SOUND: silent e

The Great Longo is lost! He wants to go home! Help him find the way home. Draw a line from the Great Longo to the first word that has the long o sound. Then draw a line to the next word with the long o sound. Pretty soon, you will get the Great Longo home!

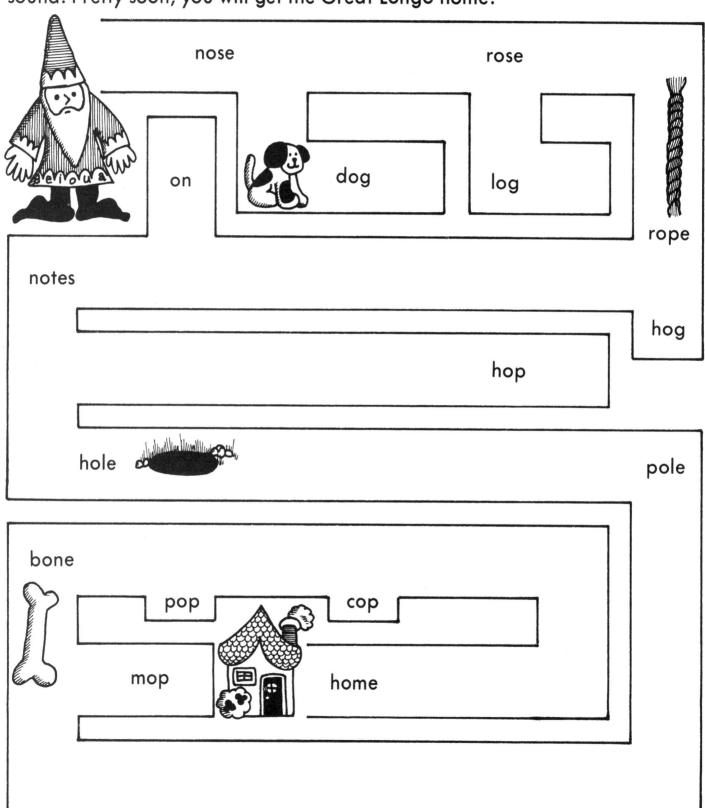

LONG O SOUND: REVIEW

Help the Great Longo put long o words inside his giant o! Look at the words at the bottom of the page. Write only the words that contain the long o sound inside Longo's o. Let's go!

Let 'em roll!

| globe | know | now | told | rode | row | rope |
| note | not | goat | get | top | home | toe |

LONG O SOUND: REVIEW

Color in each space that contains a long o word. The Great Longo has a secret message waiting for you!

				log		cat		skate
bee	bump	dog		chip				date

(grid puzzle with words: bee, bump, dog, log, chip, cat, skate, date, rate, jump, globe, lip, go, hat, not, low, so, bowl, hoe, row, lot, knee, roll, old, ship, no, late, night, toe, note, goat, hose, rode, own, blow, ice, gone, son, nice, dip, light, save)

Longo's secret message reads: _____

LONG U SOUND: silent e, ui, ew, ue

Draw a line from the long u word to the right picture. Then write the word next to the picture.

tube

_____

suit

_____

cube

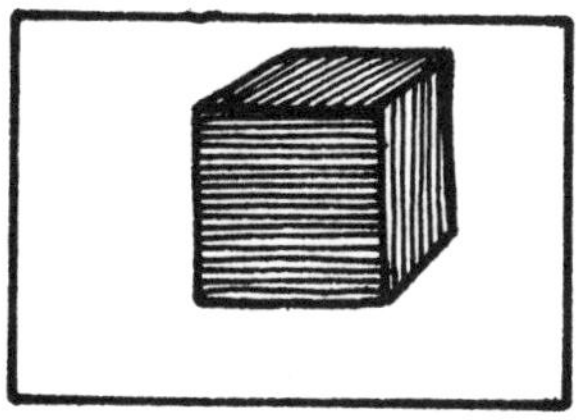

_____

fuel

_____

glue

_____

Hooray for u!

mule

_____

screw

_____

27

LONG U SOUND: REVIEW

The Great Longo has made up some riddles. Each riddle can be answered by a long u word! The words are at the bottom of the page. Write the correct word on each line.

1. If there aren't many, there are _____.

2. Standing on a mountain top,
   you have a nice _____.

3. An elephant is a _____ animal.

4. I thought that baby was very _____.

5. I heard the kitten _____.

6. When you work with something,
   you _____ it.

| mew | huge | few | view | cute | use |

LONG VOWEL SOUNDS: GENERAL REVIEW

Circle the word in each row that has the same long vowel sound as the first word in the row.

mule	lip	fuel	hot
go	clam	nut	post
chief	milk	me	fun
five	sky	stick	gift
cane	way	fan	end
leave	step	key	miss
know	fast	float	dock
rice	mile	trick	dish

LONG VOWEL SOUNDS: GENERAL REVIEW

Let's color Longo! Use the sound key to color the big picture of Longo.

Long a - - black
Long e - - red
Long i - - brown
Long o - - green
Long u - - blue

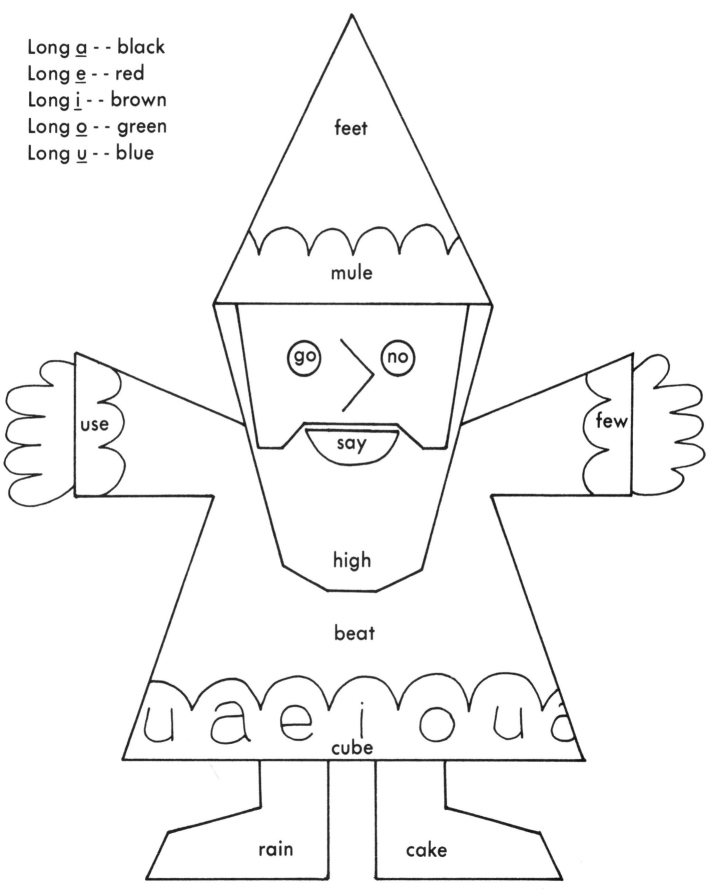

LONG VOWEL SOUNDS: GENERAL REVIEW

The Great Longo likes to play Long Vowel Opposites. You can play, too! Look at each word. Next to it, write a long vowel word that means the opposite! Use the words from the bottom of the page.

1. dirty _ _ _ _ _

2. hot _ _ _ _

3. sour _ _ _ _ _

4. you _ _

5. black _ _ _ _ _ _

6. under _ _ _ _ _

7. day _ _ _ _ _

8. wake _ _ _ _ _

9. come _ _

10. sun _ _ _ _ _

11. wet _ _ _

12. high _ _ _ _

Is the opposite of Longo... shorto?

sleep	clean	dry	cold	white	night
rain	go	over	low	sweet	me

ANSWER KEY — LONG VOWELS

Page 3
train snail rain
sail tail pail

Page 4
hay spray pray crayon
tray jay May

Page 5
1. eight
2. weigh
3. weight
4. freight
5. eight

Page 6
Automatic fill in.

Page 7
1. hate
2. pane
3. cane
4. pale
5. plane

Page 8
play
tail
plane
cake
weigh
cane
train
say
eight
pail

Page 9
stay
rain
made
take
day
bake
pail
gray

Page 10
Automatic fill in.

Page 12
Automatic fill in.

Page 11
meat   leaf   seal
peanut eagle   wheat
beak   sea   seat

Page 13
cookie
chief
she
field
he
priest
thief

Page 14
Automatic fill in.

Page 15
thief, yes   sheep, yes   bed, no
peach, yes   net, no   feet, yes
men, no   bee, yes   monkey, yes

Page 16
fly, sky
spy, sly
my, shy
lie, die
pie, tie
try, cry

Page 17
light
high
fright
knight
night
thigh
fight

Page 18
1. wild
2. child
3. mind
4. blind
5. find
6. kind

Page 19
Automatic fill in.

Page 20
bike
lie
write
might
fire
sky
wife
sight
pie
ice

Page 21
fly
pie
bike
tire
pipe
dime
knight
five

Page 22
toe   hoe   doe
road coat toast
boat goat toad

Page 23
1. go
2. bowl
3. snow
4. gold
5. ghost
6. crow
7. no
8. old

Page 24
nose
rose
rope
notes
hole
pole
bone
home

Page 25
globe
know
told
rode
row
rope
note
goat
home
toe

Page 26
old   hoe
go   roll
hose   bowl
no   note
own   goat
toe   rode
so   globe
blow
low
row
(hello)

Page 27
Automatic fill in.

Page 28
1. few
2. view
3. huge
4. cute
5. mew
6. use

Page 29
fuel
post
me
sky
way
key
float
mile

Page 30
Automatic fill in.

Page 31
1. clean
2. cold
3. sweet
4. me
5. white
6. over
7. night
8. sleep
9. go
10. rain
11. dry
12. low

SHORT A WORDS

Short a sounds like the a in apple.
It also sounds like the a in ant.

Say the picture word. Write the word. Add the correct letters.

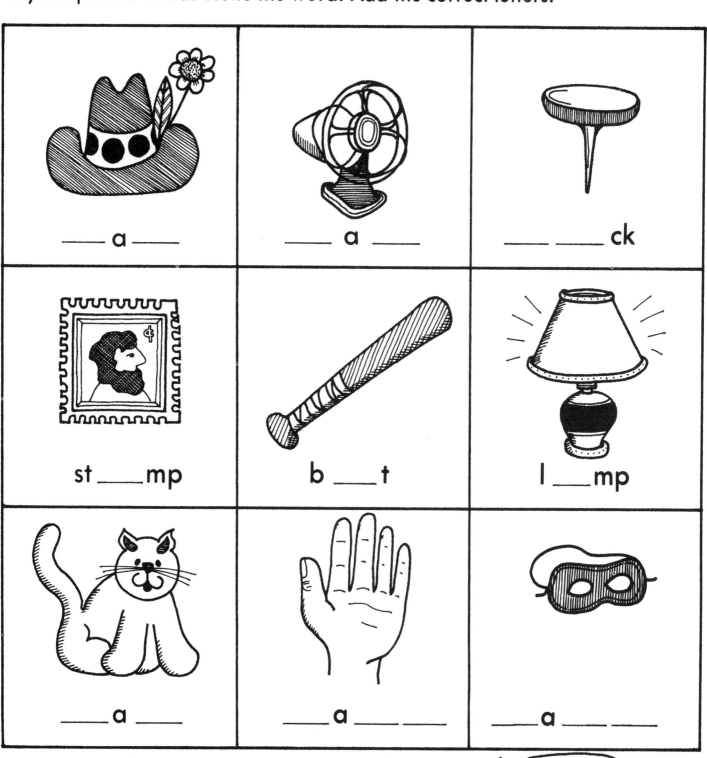

__ __ a __ __	__ __ a __	__ __ __ ck
st __ mp	b __ __ t	l __ mp
__ __ a __	__ __ a __ __	__ __ a __ __ __

My Aunt Ann is an ant who eats apples.

SHORT <u>A</u> WORDS

Say the picture word. Does the word have a short <u>a</u> sound? Circle <u>Yes</u> if it does. Circle <u>No</u> if it does not.

No	Yes No	Yes No
Yes No	Yes No	Yes No
Yes No	Yes No	Yes No
Yes No	Yes No	Yes No

Color all the words that have a short <u>a</u> sound red.

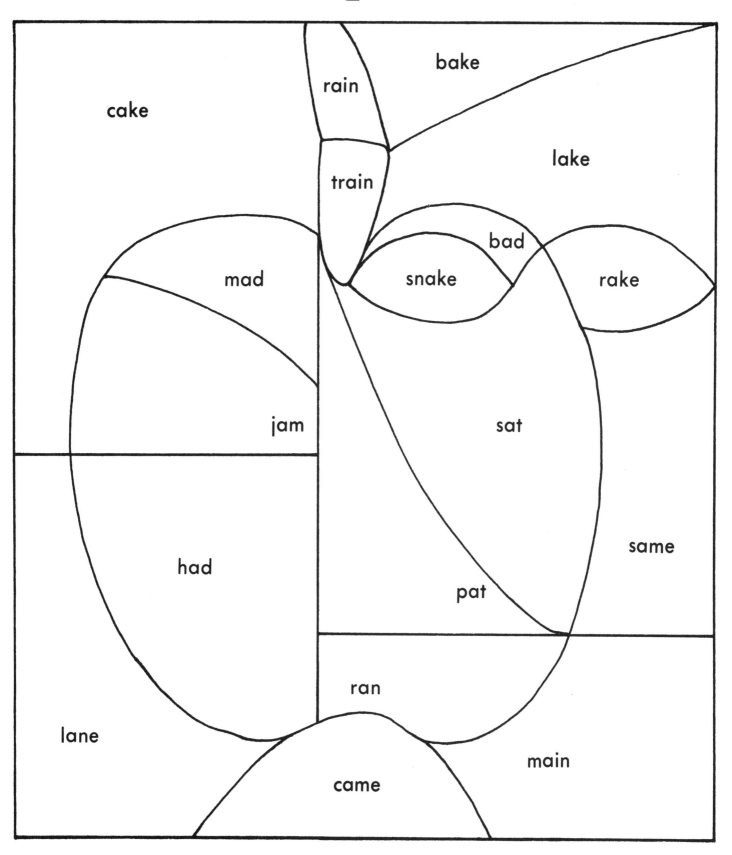

This is a picture of an ___ ___ ___ ___ ___ .

SHORT <u>A</u> WORDS

Answer the riddle. Write the correct word on the line. Then draw a picture of your answer.

mask	bat	hand	fan	cat

1. You need a ball and _____ to play baseball.

2. A _____ blows air on you.

3. On Halloween, you could wear a _____ .

4. The mother of a kitten is a _____ .

5. Hold my _____ when we cross the street.

SHORT E WORDS

Short e sounds like the first sound in Edward Elephant.

Help Edward Elephant find his way home. Write the correct short e word by each picture.

| tent | nest | sled | bell | ten | bed |

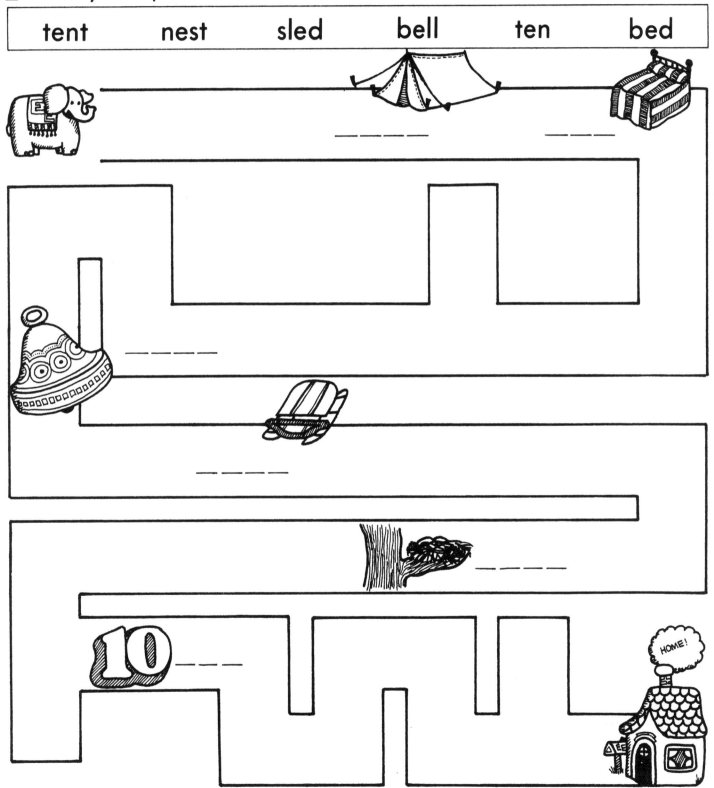

HOME!

SHORT E WORDS

Draw a line from the short e word to the correct picture. Write each word under the picture.

leg

_ _ _ _

belt

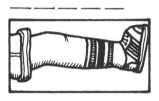

_ _ _ _

pen

_ _ _ _

dress

_ _ _ _

desk

_ _ _ _

hen

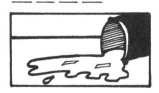

_ _ _ _

wet

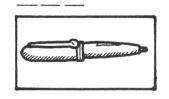

_ _ _ _

Edward Elephant has a lot of words! Some of them have the short e sound. Put an x next to the words that have the short e sound.

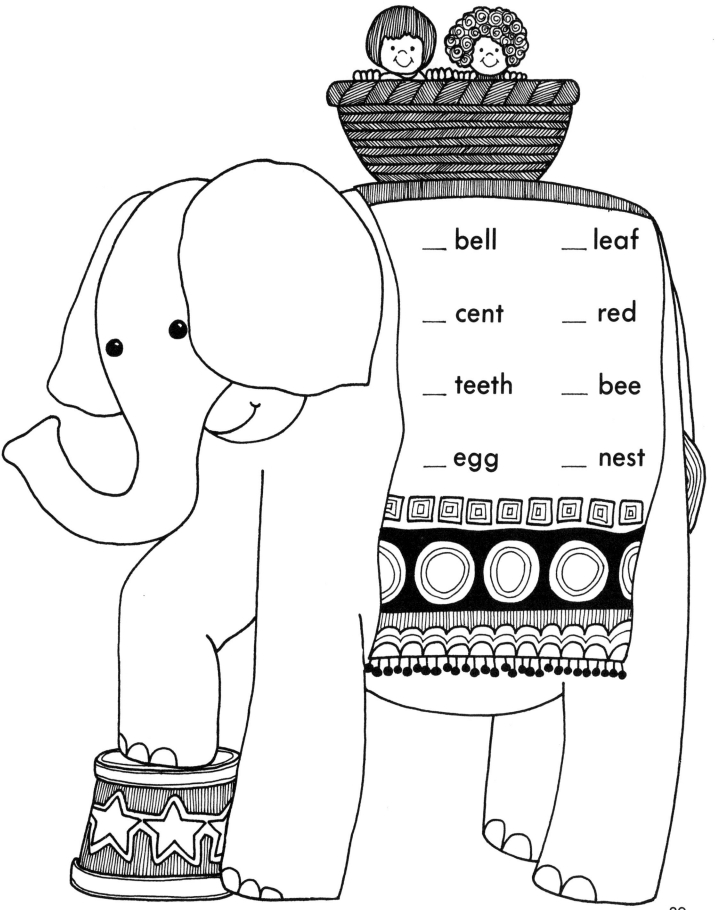

__ bell   __ leaf

__ cent   __ red

__ teeth   __ bee

__ egg   __ nest

REVIEW: <u>a</u>, <u>e</u>

Answer the riddle. Add an <u>a</u> or an <u>e</u> to get the correct answer.
Say the word.

1. You cook food in this.   p ___ n

2. You write with this.   p ___ n

3. It makes a ringing sound.   b ___ ll

4. It is a good fruit.   ___ pple

5. It is a bright color.   r ___ d

6. It lays eggs.   h ___ n

7. You hit a ball with this.   b ___ t

8. This has five fingers on it.   h ___ nd

REVIEW: <u>a</u>, <u>e</u>

Write <u>a</u> in the space if it is a short <u>a</u> word. Write <u>e</u> if it is a short <u>e</u> word. Say the word. Then draw a line from the word to the picture.

1. t ___ n

2. f ___ n

3. ___ pple

4. ___ nt

5. m ___ n

6. t ___ nt

7. d ___ sk

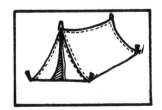

41

SHORT I WORDS

Short i sounds like the i in it.

Look at the picture. Say the word. Write in the missing letters.
Say the word again.

b __ b   f ___ sh   p __ g

__ i __ __   __ i __ __ __   __ t

l __ d   w ___ g   g __ ft

SHORT I WORDS

Look at the picture. Say the picture word. If it has a short i sound, circle Yes. If it does not have a short i sound, circle No.

Yes No	Yes No	Yes No
Yes No	Yes No	Yes No
Yes No	Yes No	Yes No
Yes No	Yes No	Yes No

SHORT I WORDS

Color all the short i words. Color them pink.

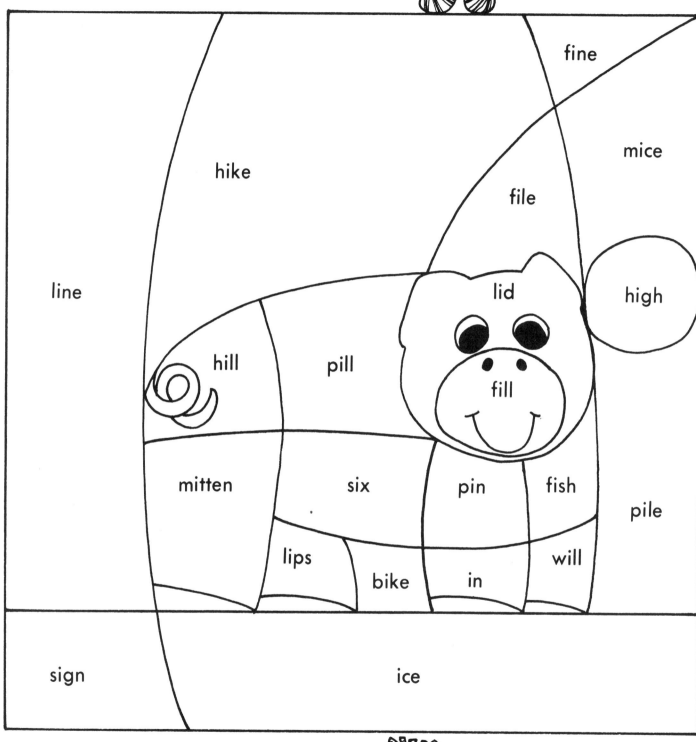

fine

mice

file

hike

line

lid

high

hill

pill

fill

mitten

six

pin

fish

pile

lips

will

bike

in

sign

ice

This is a picture of a ____ ____ ____ .

REVIEW: <u>a, i</u>

Ant and It have their words all mixed up! Write the words that have a short <u>a</u> sound in Ant's house. Write the words that have a short <u>i</u> sound in It's house.

pig	hat	lamp	six
hill	hand	fish	bad

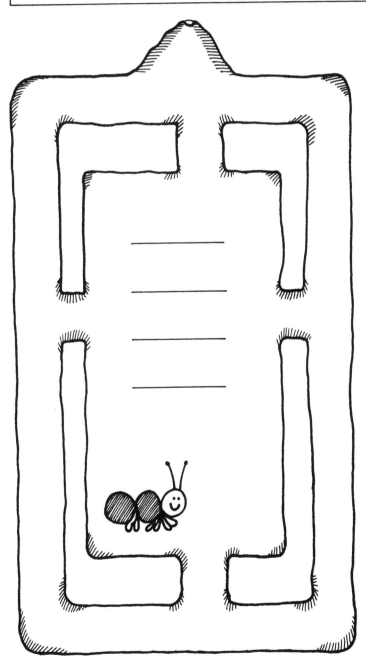

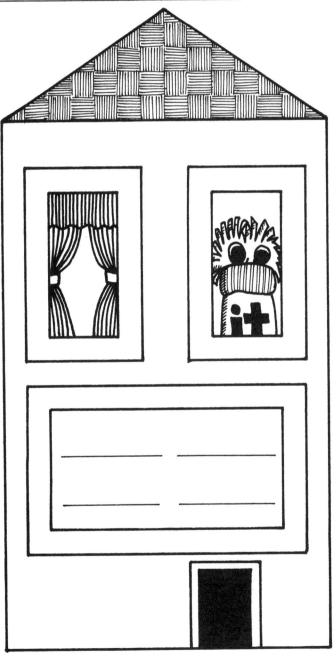

REVIEW: e, i

Help Edward Elephant and It stop fighting! Draw a line from Edward Elephant to the things that have a short e sound. Draw a line from It to the things that have a short i sound.

The sled belongs to (It, Edward Elephant).

REVIEW: <u>a</u>, <u>e</u>, <u>i</u>

There are six things hidden in the picture. Circle each hidden thing.
Write the word on the correct line.

bat	gift	pen	tent	fan	fish

Short <u>a</u> sound   Short <u>e</u> sound   Short <u>i</u> sound

_____   _____   _____

_____   _____   _____

SHORT O WORDS

Short o sounds like the beginning sound in Olive Octopus.

Olive Octopus has something in each arm! But she forgot what she has!
Put an o in each blank. Then Olive Octopus will know what she is
holding!

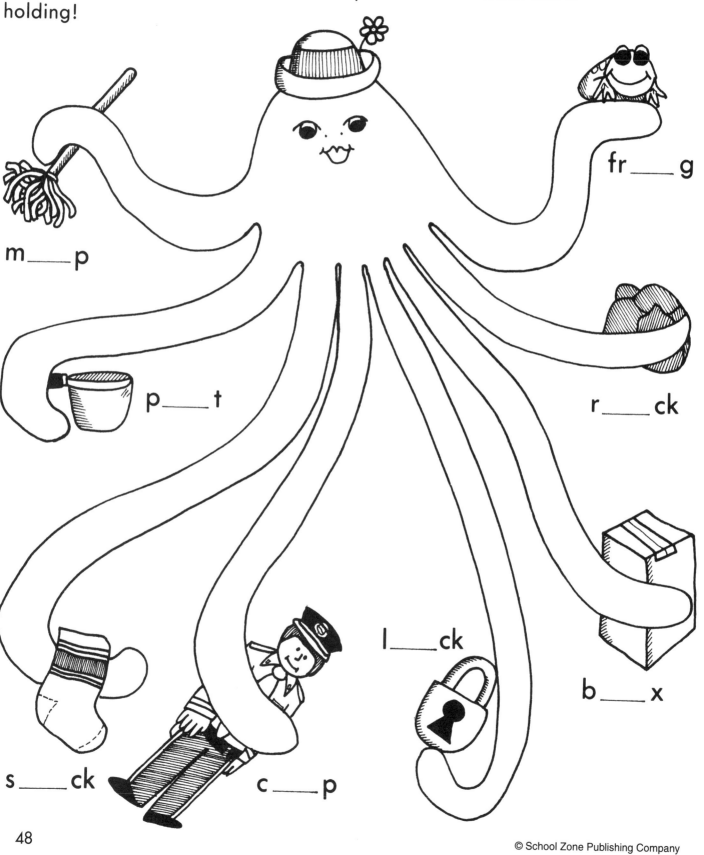

fr___g

m___p

p___t

r___ck

l___ck

b___x

s___ck

c___p

SHORT O WORDS

Circle the picture in each row whose word has a short o sound.

1.			
2.			
3.			
4.			
5.			
6.			
7.			

I like to be handy!

Color all the words that have a short _o_ sound red.

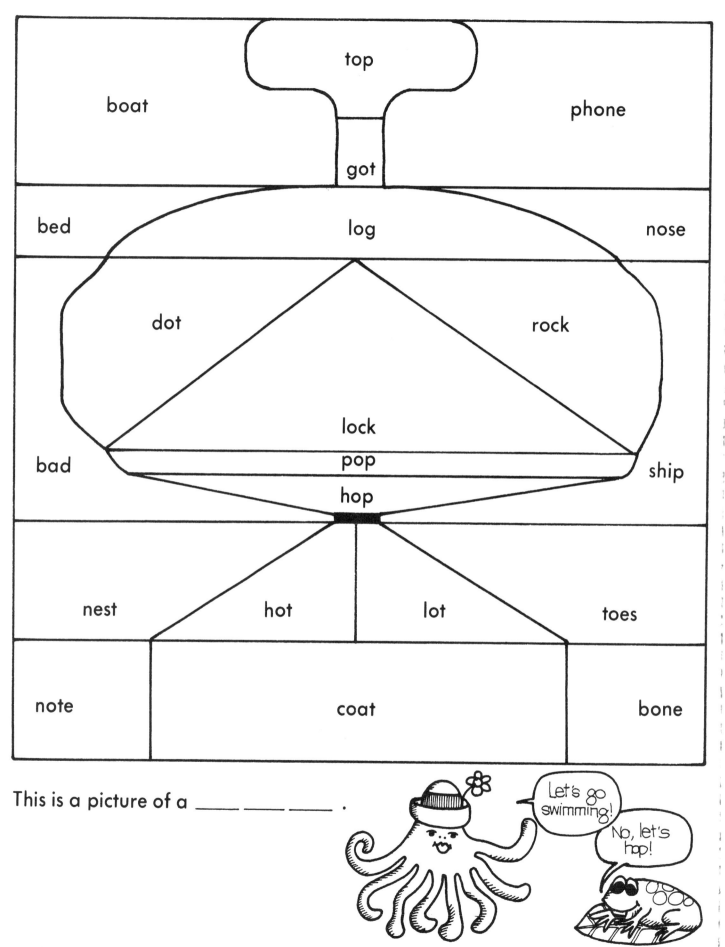

top

boat

phone

got

bed

log

nose

dot

rock

lock

pop

bad

ship

hop

nest

hot

lot

toes

note

coat

bone

This is a picture of a _____ _____ _____ .

Let's go swimming!

No, let's hop!

REVIEW: <u>a</u>, <u>o</u>

Answer the riddle. Write an <u>a</u> or an <u>o</u> in the blank. Say the word.

1. You wear this on your head.　　h＿＿t

2. A fire feels like this.　　h＿＿t

3. You play with it.　　bl＿＿ck

4. This is a color.　　bl＿＿ck

5. A drawing of the world.　　m＿＿p

6. You clean the floor with this.　　m＿＿p

7. You put it on your foot.　　s＿＿ck

8. You carry things in it.　　s＿＿ck

My, my! I hope they don't mix us up!

REVIEW: e, o

There are six hidden things in the picture. Draw a line around each thing. Then write the words below.

| clock | bell | hen | pot | bed | mop |

Short e words

_____

_____

_____

Short o words

_____

_____

_____

REVIEW: i, o

Look at each picture. Say the picture word. Circle i if the word has a short i sound. Circle o if the word has a short o sound.

i o	i o	i o
i o	i o	i o
i o	i o	i o

53

REVIEW: <u>a</u>, <u>e</u>, <u>i</u>, <u>o</u>

Circle the picture in each row that has the short vowel sound.

short a			
short e			
short e			
short i			
short a			
short o			
short i			
short o			

SHORT U WORDS

Short u sounds like the first sound of Uppity Up.

Look at the picture. Say the picture word. Write the missing letters on the line. Say the word.

c ___ p   b ___ s   b ___ g

___ U ___   ___ ___ U ___   ___ U ___

g ___ m   s ___ b   br ___ sh

Uppity Up has lost his words! Circle the pictures that have a short <u>u</u> sound. They belong to Uppity Up.

56

Color all the short u words orange.

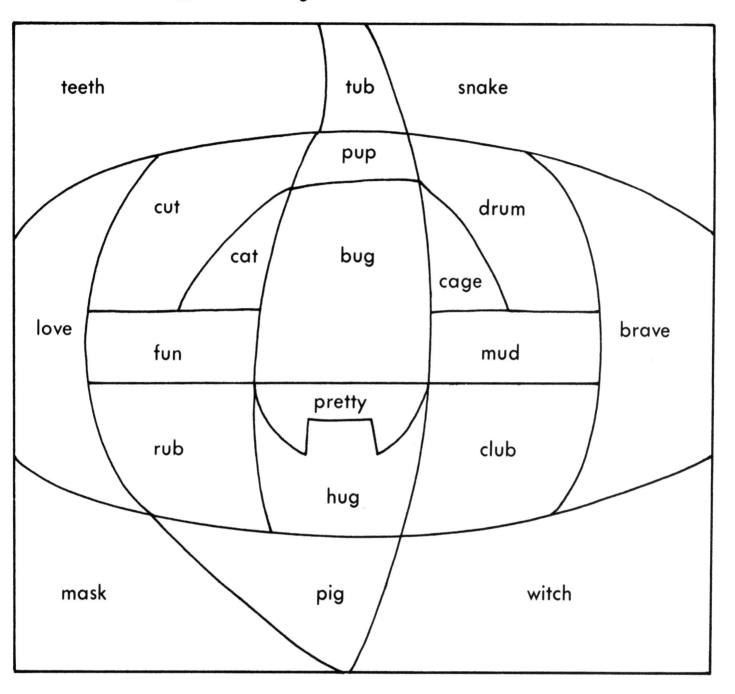

teeth

tub

snake

pup

cut

drum

cat

bug

cage

love

fun

mud

brave

pretty

rub

club

hug

mask

pig

witch

This is a (sun, bus, pumpkin).

It looks all wrong to me!

REVIEW: <u>a</u>, <u>u</u>

Answer the riddle. Write <u>a</u> or <u>u</u> on the line. Say the word.

1. It goes on your head. c＿＿p

2. You drink from it. c＿＿p

3. It is wet dirt. m＿＿d

4. It means the same as angry. m＿＿d

5. It is small. b＿＿g

6. You can keep a lunch in it. b＿＿g

7. It blows cool air. f＿＿n

8. You have this when you play. f＿＿n

Uppity up is stuck up!

REVIEW: e, u

Circle the words or pictures that have the sound in the box.

Short e	Short u
	hug lot tub
Short e bet feet lips tent	**Short u**

REVIEW: i, u

Draw a line from the letter to a picture that has the short vowel sound.

60

REVIEW: <u>o</u>, <u>u</u>

Help Olive Octopus and Uppity Up find their way home. Write the correct word by the picture.

REVIEW: a̱, e̱, i̱, o̱, u̱

Add a short vowel to make a word. Then write the words on the correct line. Say each word.

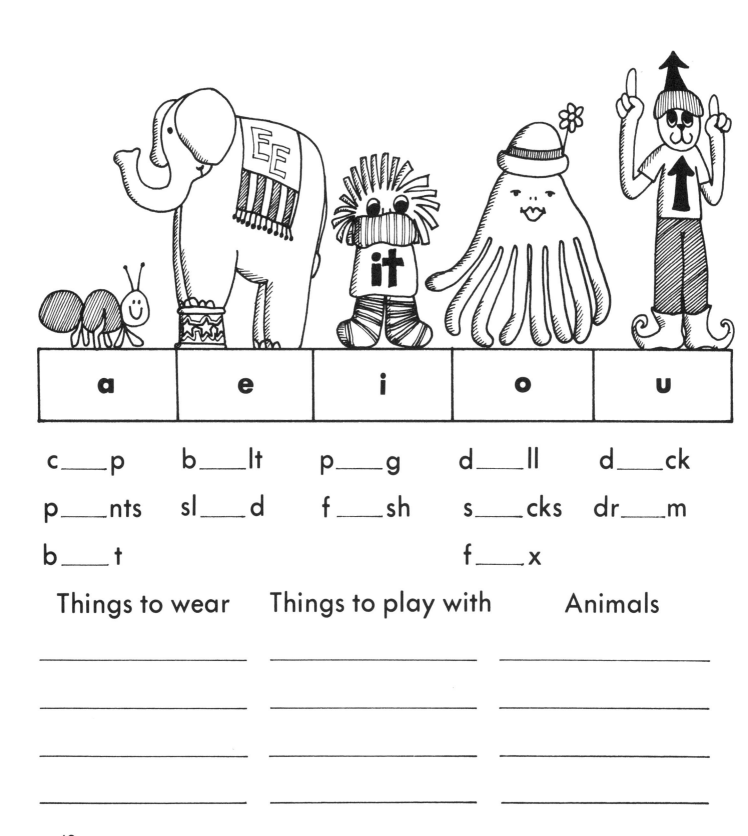

a	e	i	o	u

c___p   b___lt   p___g   d___ll   d___ck

p___nts   sl___d   f___sh   s___cks   dr___m

b___t   f___x

Things to wear   Things to play with   Animals

_____   _____   _____

_____   _____   _____

_____   _____   _____

_____   _____   _____

REVIEW: <u>a</u>, <u>e</u>, <u>i</u>, <u>o</u>, <u>u</u>

Look at the picture. Say the picture word. Circle the short vowel that has the same sound as the picture word.

ANSWER KEY — SHORT VOWELS

Page 33

hat	fan	tack
stamp	bat	lamp
cat	hand	mask

Page 34

train-no
bag-yes
fan-yes
rake-no
rain-no
lamp-yes
ant-yes
man-yes
cake-no
lamb-yes
snake-no
cat-yes

Page 35

ran
bad
had
mad
sat
pat
jam
(apple)

Page 36

1. bat
2. fan
3. mask
4. cat
5. hand

Page 37

tent
bed
bell
sled
nest
ten

Page 38

dress
leg
hen
belt
desk
wet
pen

Page 39

bell	red
cent	nest
egg	

Page 40

1. pan
2. pen
3. bell
4. apple
5. red
6. hen
7. bat
8. hand

Page 41

1. ten
2. fan
3. apple
4. ant
5. man
6. tent
7. desk

Page 42

bib	fish	pig
dish	hill	It
lid	wig	gift

Page 43

fish-yes
slide-no
six-yes
kite-no
fire-no
witch-yes
lid-yes
lips-yes
pie-no
ship-yes
pig-yes
dish-yes

Page 44

fish
pin
six
mitten
lips
in
will
pill
hill
lid
fill
(pig)

Page 45

Short a words
hat
hand
lamp
bad

Short i words
pig
six
hill
fish

Page 46

Short e words
dress
tent
leg
ten

Short i words
lips
ship
dish
six

Sled belongs to
Edward Elephant.

Page 47

1. Short a - bat, fan
2. Short e - pen, tent
3. Short i - gift, fish

Page 48

Automatic fill in.

Page 49

1. sock
2. clock
3. fox
4. top
5. mop
6. block
7. cop

Page 50

top
log
dot
rock
got
lock
hot
lot
hop
pop
(top)

Page 51

1. hat
2. hot
3. block
4. black
5. map
6. mop
7. sock
8. sack

Page 52

Short e words
bell, hen, bed

Short o words
clock, pot, mop

Page 53

ship, i
witch, i
cop, o
fox, o
socks, o
mittens, i
clock, o
six, i
pot, o

Page 54

Short a - hand
Short e - belt
Short e - desk
Short i - pig
Short a - bat
Short o - lock
Short i - bib
Short o - dog

Page 55

cup	bus	bug
sun	drum	duck
gum	sub	brush

Page 56

sun
drum
duck
tub
hut
cup

Page 57

pup
mud
fun
hug
bug
tub
club
rub
drum
cut
(pumpkin)

Page 58

1. cap
2. cup
3. mud
4. mad
5. bug
6. bag
7. fan
8. fun

Page 59

Short e — desk, nest
Short u — hug, tub
Short e — bet, tent
Short u — truck, duck

Page 60

Short i words
pig
witch
fish
mittens

Short u words
bus
cup
duck
drum

Page 61

mop
cop
bus
lock
duck
fox

Page 62

Things to wear
cap
pants
belt
socks

Things to play with
bat
sled
doll
drum

Animals
pig
fox
fish
duck

Page 63

desk-e
lips-i
octopus-o
duck-u
cat-a
elephant-e
pig-i
nest-e
six-i
cup-u
ant-a
ship-i
drum-u
hand-a
fox-o
It-i

Answer the riddle. The answer to each riddle rhymes with cat.

pat
hat
bat
sat
rat

1. Fat Cat plays ball with this.
   It is a ___ ___ ___.

2. Fat Cat runs after this.
   It is a ___ ___ ___.

3. People do this to Fat Cat. Then he purrs.
   They ___ ___ ___.

4. Fat Cat wears one on his head.
   It is a ___ ___ ___.

5. Fat Cat did this when he was tired.
   He ___ ___ ___.

Read the sentence. Circle the words that rhyme. Then draw a picture.

The fish was in the dish.

The goat in the boat wore a coat.

Read the word in the box. Circle the picture that rhymes with the word. Write the name of the picture on the line.

thing

sing

sing

thing

_____

_____

_____

_____

Here is a story about Jake. Circle every word that rhymes with Jake.

Jake liked to bake. What should he make?

He would make a cake! A cake is what Jake would bake! Jake made the cake. He put it in to bake.

Then he went out. Jake went to the lake. He picked up a rake. Poor Jake! You cannot rake a lake!

But Jake said the lake was fake! He said he would take the rake. Take the rake and make a lake!

Jake! Stop, for goodness' sake! Go and check your cake! Forget about the fake lake!

I don't think Jake is awake!

68

Read the words. Write each word next to the correct picture. Say the word out loud.

book	cook	hook	look	took

_____

_____

_____

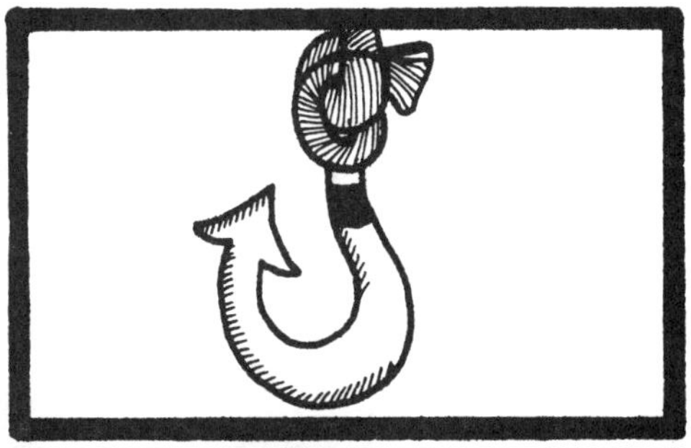

_____

_____

Look at the picture. Circle the word that names the picture.

let
pet
met

let
bet
net

vet
met
bet

net
pet
met

I'll bet the vet has a net to catch a pet.

70

Play tick-tack-toe. Draw a line through the three words that rhyme.
Then write the three rhyming words on the line.

well	bend	send
boat	coat	goat
toy	look	dime

_____

_____

_____

wish	cake	log
right	fish	cold
rake	bill	dish

_____

_____

_____

thing	dog	hook
ring	time	coat
sing	cat	make

_____

_____

_____

fish	like	sat
take	mat	ball
bat	bike	log

_____

_____

_____

71

Read each sentence. Write the correct word on the line.

1. A _____ is green.
   dog   hog   frog

2. The _____ ran after the ball.
   dog   log   hog

3. A _____ is a big pig.
   frog   dog   hog

4. The woman cut the _____ with a saw.
   log   hog   frog

The frog sat on a log in the bog.

Say the word. Circle the picture that rhymes with the word.

big	
den	
fig	
pen	
big	
den	

Say the words. Draw a line from the words to the correct picture.

1. bed

2. sled

3. Ned and Ted

4. Ned fled.

5. Ned, Ted, and Jed

6. Ted led Jed.

Ned fled on a sled. Ted led Jed to another sled.

Make your own poem! Fill in the blanks with the words given.

town   Brown   crown   gown   down

Brenda _____
Went to _____.
She bought a _____
And a _____.

Brenda _____
Fell right _____.
She tore her _____
And broke her _____.

Read each sentence. Two words in each sentence rhyme. Circle the two words that rhyme.

1. The ball went over the wall.

2. The wall was tall.

3. Did you fall in the hall?

4. Did the ball fall on the cat?

5. She will call over the wall.

6. We play ball in the fall.

Read each word. Draw a line from the word to the correct picture.

1. jam

2. ham

3. Sam

4. Sam and ram

5. Sam and ham

6. Sam at the dam

Sam spread the jam on the ham, and fed it to the ram!

Look at the picture. Say the picture word. Circle the word that names the picture.

fat mat cat	bake cake lake	dish wish fish	king thing swing
goat boat coat	fall hall ball	wall tall call	sled bed red
brown gown crown	pig wig dig	bake take lake	hen pen men
ten men hen	dog frog hog	net pet let	look book cook

Answer the riddle. Write the correct word on the line.

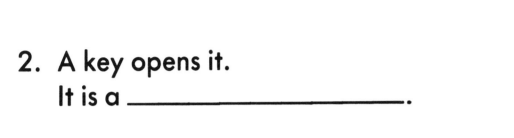

block   clock   lock   dock   sock

1. It tells you the time.
   It is a _____.

2. A key opens it.
   It is a _____.

3. You wear it on your foot.
   It is a _____.

4. You play with it.
   It is a _____.

5. A boat can be here.
   It is a _____.

If it goes tick **tock** it is a clock.

Read the sound in the box. Circle the word or picture that rhymes with the sound in the box.

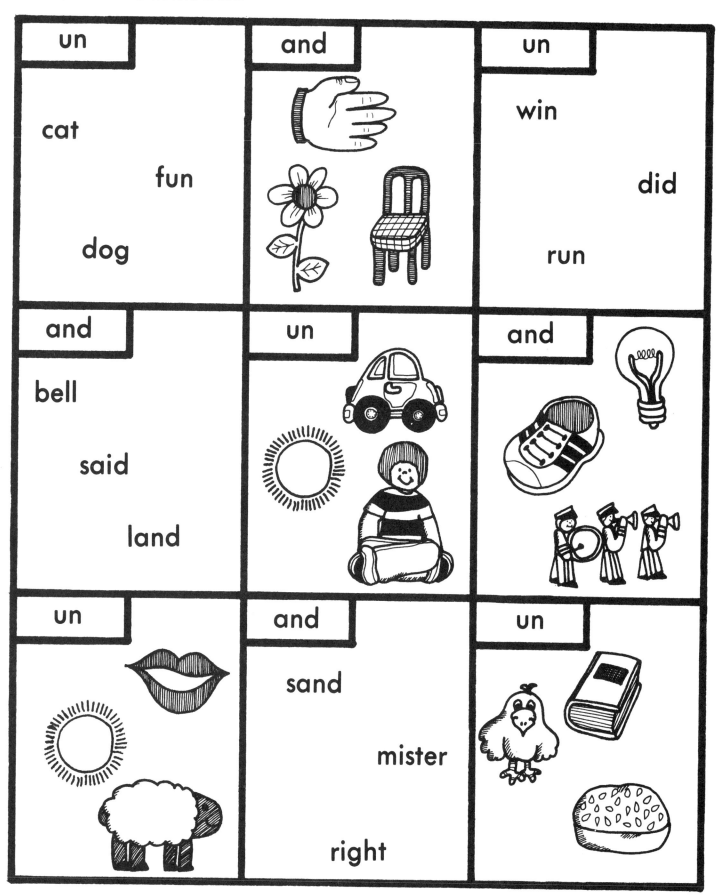

un	and	un
cat fun dog		win did run

and	un	and
bell said land		

un	and	un
	sand mister right	

Read each sentence. Write the correct word on the line.

1. Jenny drank the _____.

   mop   pop   hop

2. Dad cleaned the floor with a _____.

   top   hop   mop

3. Mike said hello to the _____.

   cop   top   hop

4. That rabbit sure can _____.

   mop   hop   cop

5. The lid of the jar is the _____.

   hop   cop   top

I'll bop down to the rabbit hop and help the cop mop!

Color blue all the words that rhyme with an.

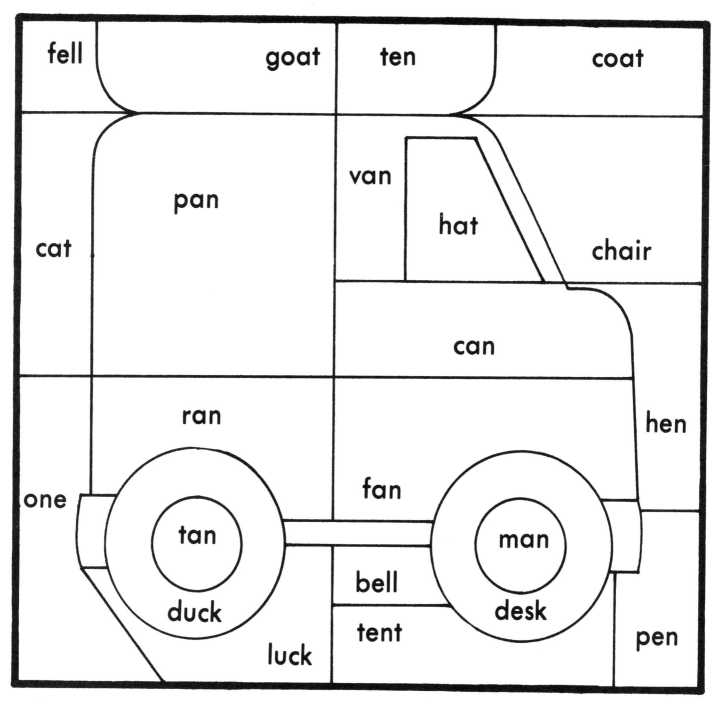

fell	goat	ten	coat
van	hat	chair	
cat	pan		
	can	hen	
	ran		
one	tan	fan	man
	duck	bell	desk
	luck	tent	pen

This is a picture of a (man fan van).

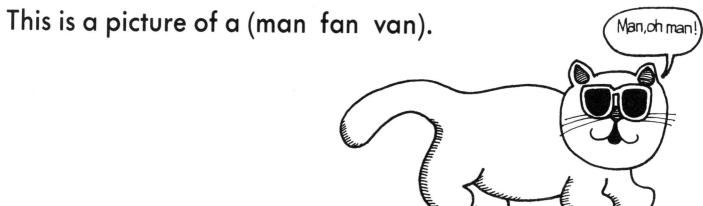

Man, oh man!

82

Mack the Hack is a Lumberjack! He wants you to have fun with the ack sound. Follow the directions.

p	cr	J	bl	b	t

1. Add one letter to ack. The word means "not in front."

   It is in _____.

2. Add two letters to ack. The word is a color.

   It is _____.

3. Add a capital letter to ack. It is a boy's name.

   It is _____.

4. Add two letters to ack. It is in a sidewalk.

   It is a _____.

5. Add one letter to ack. It is very sharp.

   It is a _____.

6. Add one letter to ack. You do this to a suitcase.

   You _____ it.

A lot of words rhyme with **old**. Find the way to the gold.
Write all the **old** words.

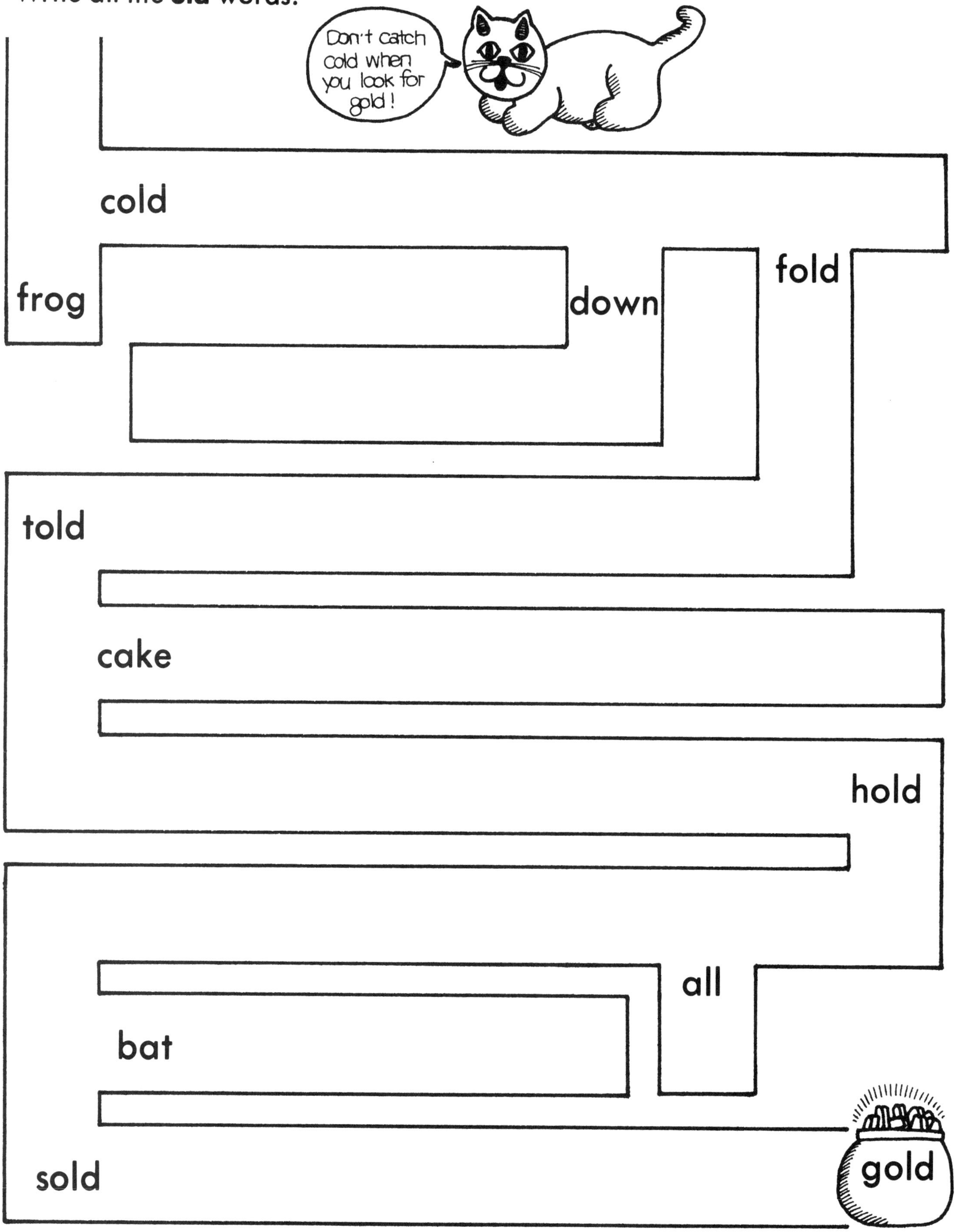

Don't catch cold when you look for gold!

cold

frog

down

fold

told

cake

hold

all

bat

sold

gold

Look at the picture. Add one letter to the first line to make a word.
The word tells what the picture is. Then add letters to the other lines
to make words that rhyme.

___ake

r ___ ___ ___

b ___ ___ ___

t ___ ___ ___

___at

b ___ ___

r ___ ___

s ___ ___

___en

p ___ ___

t ___ ___

m ___ ___

___all

f ___ ___ ___

t ___ ___ ___

c ___ ___ ___

___an

f ___ ___

m ___ ___

r ___ ___

___ook

t ___ ___ ___

l ___ ___ ___

c ___ ___ ___

Draw a line from the word to the correct picture. Say each word.

dot

Spot

pot

knot

hot

Scott

Read the sentence. Circle the words that rhyme. Then draw a picture.

Nell fell in the well.

Yell when I ring the bell.

Look at the words. Write a word next to the correct picture. Say the word.

| lap | cap | trap | map | nap |

_____

_____

_____

_____

_____

I like to wear a cap when I take a nap.

Help the jay hide in the hay! Write all the words that rhyme with jay and hay on the lines.

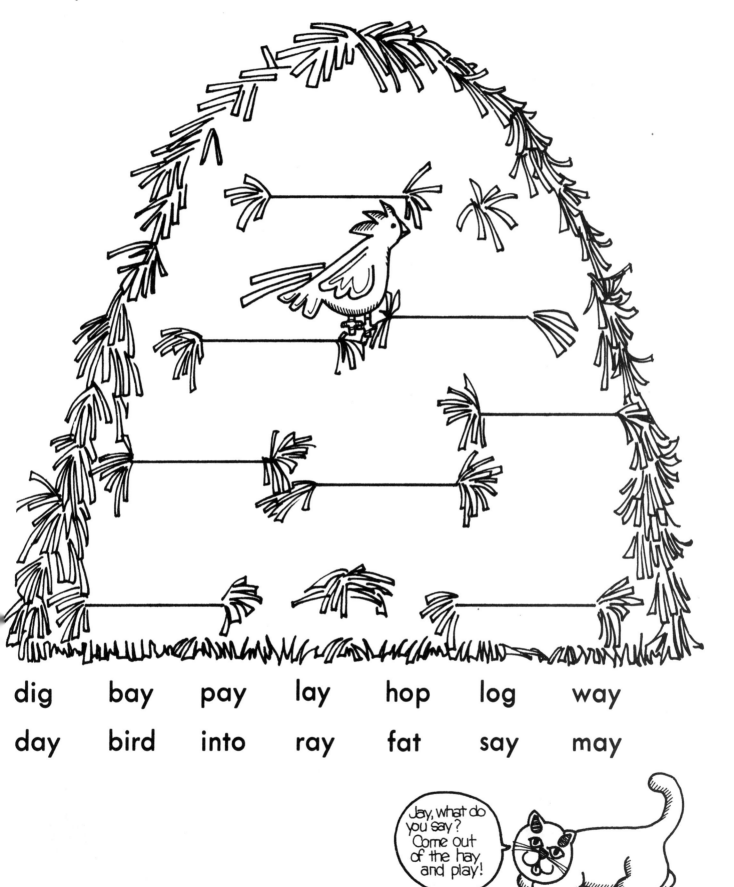

dig   bay   pay   lay   hop   log   way

day   bird   into   ray   fat   say   may

Jay, what do you say? Come out of the hay and play!

This is a story about Bug. Fill in the lines with the correct words. All the words rhyme with Bug.

1. Bug liked to sleep on a _____.

2. Bug drank her milk from a _____.

3. When Bug liked somebody, she gave them a _____.

4. One day Bug saw a long rope. She gave it a _____.

   Oops! Dirt dropped on Bug!

5. Bug had to get out! So Bug _____ her way out.

6. Then she went home. Bug went back to sleep on her _____.

This is a tent game. Write all the words that rhyme with tent on the lines.

The tent vent is bent!

rent go bent cent away dent chair bird sent

REVIEW

Look at the pictures. Say the picture words. Circle <u>Yes</u> if the picture words rhyme. Circle <u>No</u> if they do not rhyme.

Yes No	Yes No
Yes No	Yes No
Yes No	Yes No
Yes No	Yes No

REVIEW

Draw a line from the rhyming words to the correct picture.

fat cat

hot pot

goat coat

wet pet

bug mug

frown clown

fish dish

bell fell

bent tent

REVIEW

Read the sentence. Say the word in the box. Then put a
box around the word that rhymes with it.

1. I fell into the ⬚well⬚.

2. ⬚Look⬚ at my new book.

3. The boy had a new ⬚toy⬚.

4. I like your red ⬚bike⬚.

5. I ⬚told⬚ you I had a cold.

6. The vet helped my ⬚pet⬚.

7. Did Nell ⬚tell⬚ you a joke?

8. Ten ⬚men⬚ went to work.

Fat Cat Sat.

REVIEW

Read each riddle. Write the answer on the line. Then draw a picture of your answer.

1. It rhymes with red.
   You sleep in it. _____

2. It rhymes with dish.
   It can swim. _____

3. It rhymes with lake.
   You eat it. _____

4. It rhymes with hall.
   It is a toy. _____

5. It rhymes with boat.
   It is something to wear. _____

6. It rhymes with tell.
   It rings. _____

It rhymes with send. This is the _____

ANSWER KEY

Page 65
1. bat
2. rat
3. pat
4. hat
5. sat

Page 66
fish-dish
goat-boat-coat

Page 67
thing-ring
sing-king
sing-wing
thing-swing

Page 68
bake, make
make, cake, cake, bake, cake, bake
lake, rake, rake, lake
lake, fake, take, rake, take,
    rake, make, lake
sake, cake, fake, lake

Page 69
cook
took
book
hook
look

Page 70
pet, net
vet, met

Page 71
boat, goat, coat
wish, fish, dish
thing, ring, sing
bat, mat, sat

Page 72
1. frog
2. dog
3. hog
4. log

Page 73
big-pig
den-hen
fig-wig
pen-men
big-dig
den-ten

Page 75
Brown,
town
gown/crown
crown/gown
Brown
down
gown
crown

Page 76
1. ball, wall
2. wall, tall
3. fall, hall
4. ball, fall
5. call, wall
6. ball, fall

Page 78
cat, cake, fish, king
coat, ball, wall, sled
crown, wig, lake, men
ten, frog, net, book

Page 79
1. clock
2. lock
3. sock
4. block
5. dock

Page 80
un-fun, and-hand, un-run
and-land, un-sun, and-band
un-sun, and-sand, un-bun

Page 81
1. pop
2. mop
3. cop
4. hop
5. top

Page 82
pan   fan
van   man
can   tan
ran   (van)

Page 83
1. back
2. black
3. Jack
4. crack
5. tack
6. pack

Page 84
cold
fold
told
hold
sold
gold

Page 85
cake   cat
rake   bat
bake   rat
take   sat

hen   ball
pen   fall
ten   tall
men   call

can   book
fan   took
man   look
ran   cook

Page 87
Nell, fell, well
yell, bell

Page 88
cap
nap
map
trap
lap

Page 89
day, bay, lay
may, pay, ray
say, way

Page 90
1. rug
2. mug
3. hug
4. tug
6. dug
7. rug

Page 91
rent, bent
cent, dent
sent

Page 92
cat-hat, yes
cake-foot, no
pig-wig, yes
hook-book, yes
log-dog, yes
bed-sled, yes
balloon-shoe, no
bug-mouse, no

Page 94
1. fell
2. book
3. boy
4. like
5. cold
6. vet
7. Nell
8. Ten

Page 95
1. bed
2. fish
3. cake
4. ball
5. coat
6. bell

96

bl

<u>Bl</u> stands for the Blue Blender! He puts letters together and makes the sounds of the letters glide together.

Help the Blue Blender make the words below. Add the right letters to make a word and answer the riddle. Then color the Blue Blender. Color his suit blue!

The color of the sky.   __ __ ue

You play with these.   __ __ ocks

The color of the night.   __ __ ack

You do this to birthday candles.   __ __ ow

cl

Cl stands for Clara Clown.
Color all the words that start with cl.

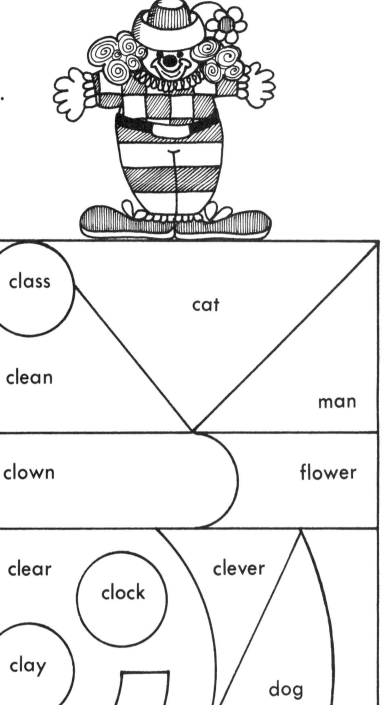

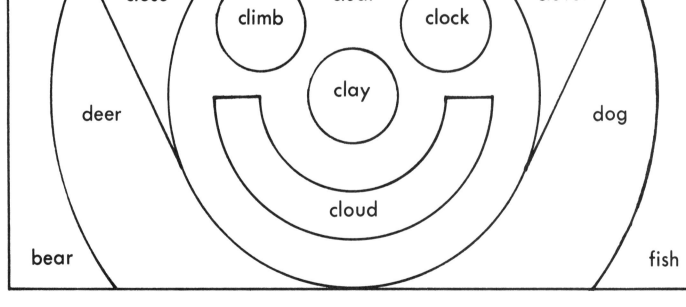

monkey

class

cat

clean

hold

man

baby

clown

flower

close

clear

clever

climb

clock

deer

clay

dog

cloud

bear

fish

The picture is of a __ __ __ __ __.

fl

Fl stands for Flora Flower.
Add fl to the words. Then draw a line from the word to the picture.

—— y

—— ag

—— oor

—— ower

—— ame

gl

GI stands for Glad Gloria!

Wait! Glad Gloria is not glad! She is sad! She is sad because she has lost three things. They all begin with gl. Help her find the things. Draw a line around them. Then write the words below.

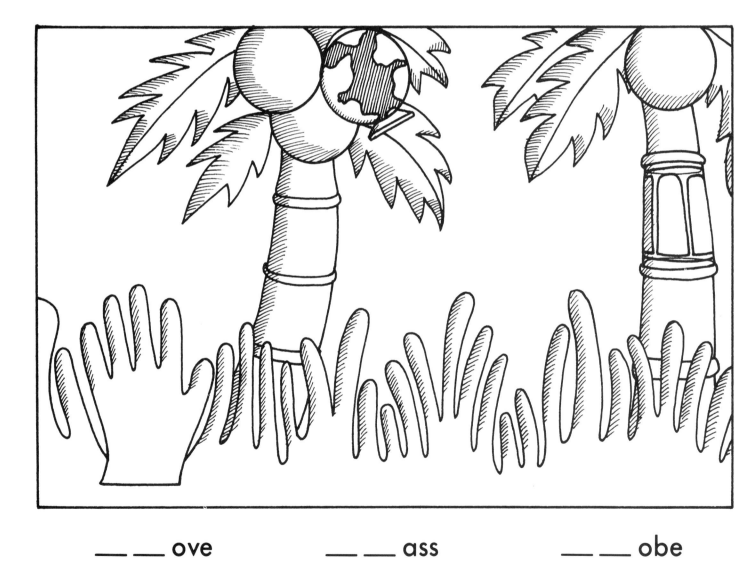

__ __ ove   __ __ ass   __ __ obe

How will Gloria feel when she finds the things she lost? __ __ __ __

pl

PI stands for please.

Circle the word that begins with pl.

1. pet   gold   plan

2. play   snake   blue

3. green   chair   plant

4. book   place   dark

5. please   clown   parade

sl

<u>Sl</u> stands for Sleepy Slim.

Draw a line around the pictures that begin with the <u>sl</u> sound.

102

REVIEW: l blends

Are you handy with blends? Let's see if you are. Write each blend once to make a new word. Say the new word.

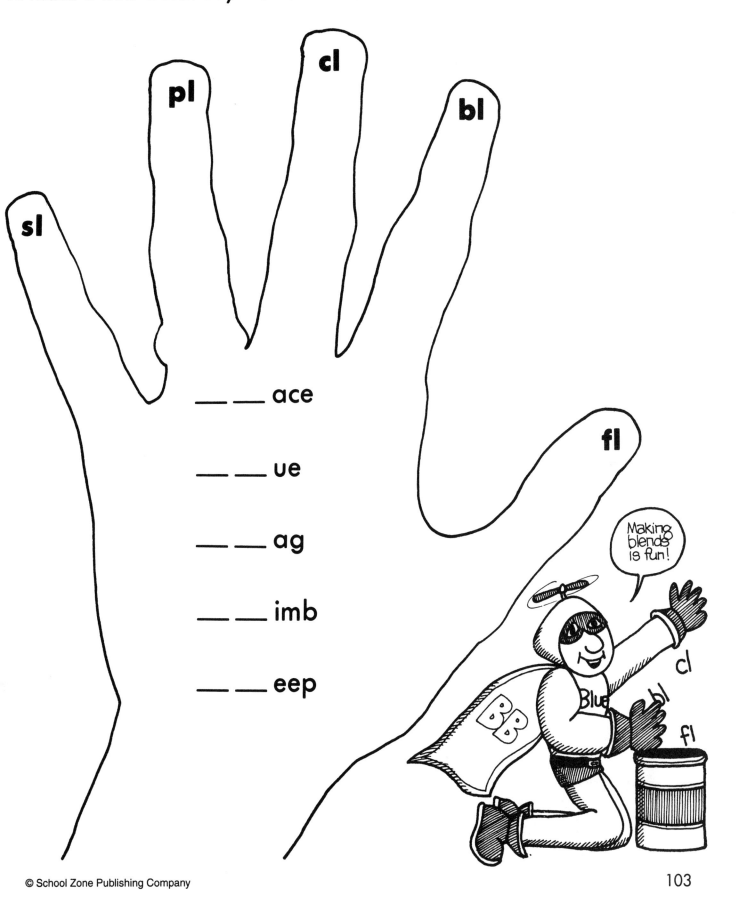

pl

cl

bl

sl

fl

___ ___ ace

___ ___ ue

___ ___ ag

___ ___ imb

___ ___ eep

Making blends is fun!

BB
Blue
cl
bl
fl

br

Br stands for branches.

Write the correct word on each branch. Say the word.

3. We had to go over a _____.

2. My _____ is six today.

1. I need a _____ and dust pan.

4. The sun was _____.

5. The man was _____.

6. The _____ fell from the tree.

branch

brave

bright

brook

broom

brother

My brother brags that he is brave.

cr

Cr stands for Crazy Crow.

Draw a line around six picture words that begin with cr.

dr

Dr stands for drivers!

Color the <u>dr</u> words green.

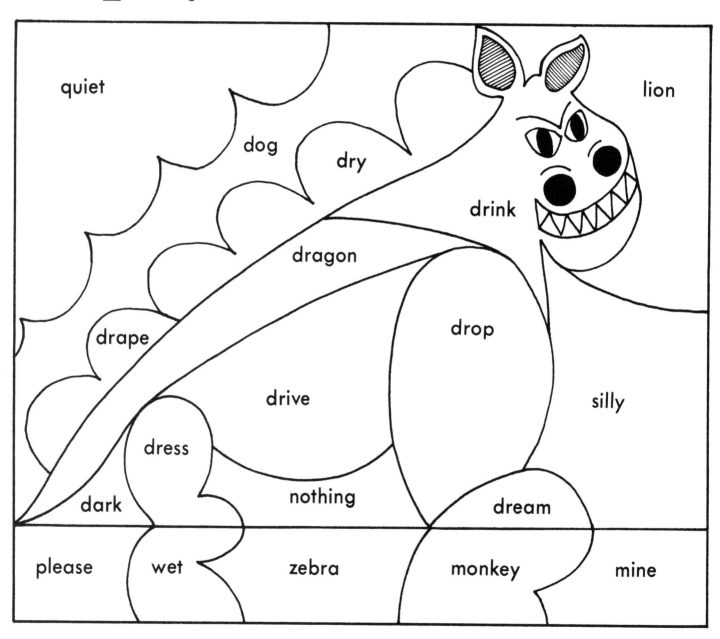

quiet

dog

dry

lion

drink

dragon

drape

drop

drive

silly

dress

dark

nothing

dream

please

wet

zebra

monkey

mine

This is a picture of a (dress dragon driver).

106

fr

Fr stands for Friendly Frog.

Friendly Frog likes to ask riddles. Read his riddles. Then write the answers.

frog	from	friend	front	fruits	frighten

1. Somebody you like is a _____.

2. It is not the back. It is the _____.

3. Suzie got a present _____ Jimmy.

4. A green animal that hops is a _____.

5. Apples, oranges, and bananas are _____.

6. If you scare somebody, you _____ them.

Here, Friendly Frog. Have some fresh fruit!

107

gr

Gr stands for green grass. Color the grass green.

Add gr to each word. Say the word.

1. __ __ een

2. __ __ ass

3. __ __ andmother

4. __ __ apes

5. __ __ asshopper

6. __ __ ill

7. __ __ andfather

pr

<u>Pr</u> stands for Proud Prince.

Connect the dots.
You will see what the Proud Prince is holding.

He is holding a (frog pretty present).

Draw a line around seven words that start with <u>pr</u>.

pretty

peanut

night

present

day

princess

prize

girl

pray

black

turtle

proud

prison

tr

Tr stands for train.

Draw a line around the blend that begins each picture word.

bl pr tr pl	tr br gl gr	cl cr bl tr
tr br gr pr	cl tr fr br	fr pl pr tr

Trudy tried a trick. She trapped a train.

110

REVIEW: r blends

Help the train go down the track. Make a word at each stop.
Use one of the blends to make a word.

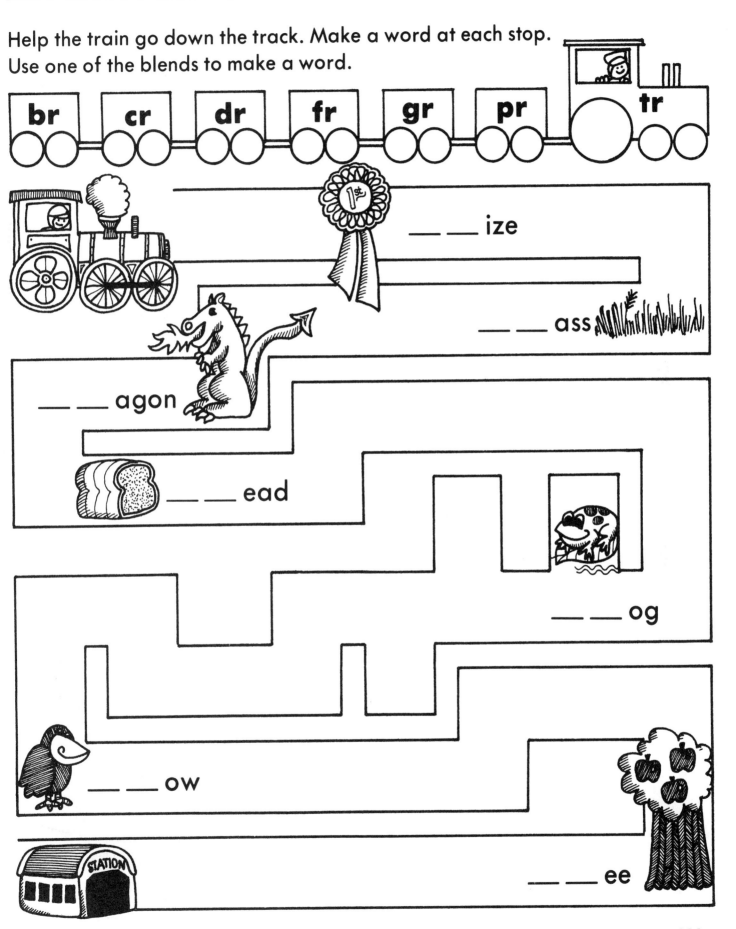

br cr dr fr gr pr tr

__ __ ize

__ __ ass

__ __ agon

__ __ ead

__ __ og

__ __ ow

__ __ ee

sw

Sw is for swim.

sp

Sp is for Spot.

Swim, Spot, swim!

Make a word. Put the right letters in front of the word.
Say the word. Draw a line from the word to the picture.

__ __ ider

__ __ im

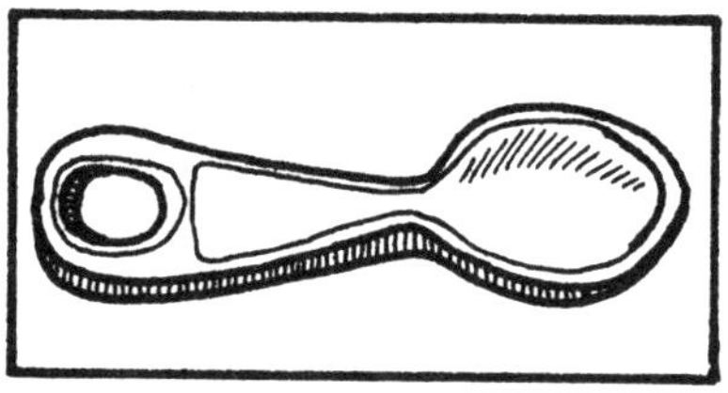

__ __ oon

__ __ an

Write two words that begin with sw.

_____

_____

Write two words that begin with sp.

_____

_____

sm

Sm is for small.

sn

Sn is for snail.

Draw a line around the picture that starts with the blend in the box.

sm			
sn			
sn			
sm			
sm			
sn			

Smart snails always smile at snakes!

st

St is for Start and Stop!

Start and Stop are lost! Help them get home. Draw a line from Start and Stop to the next st word. Then to the next. If you follow the st words, Start and Stop will get home.

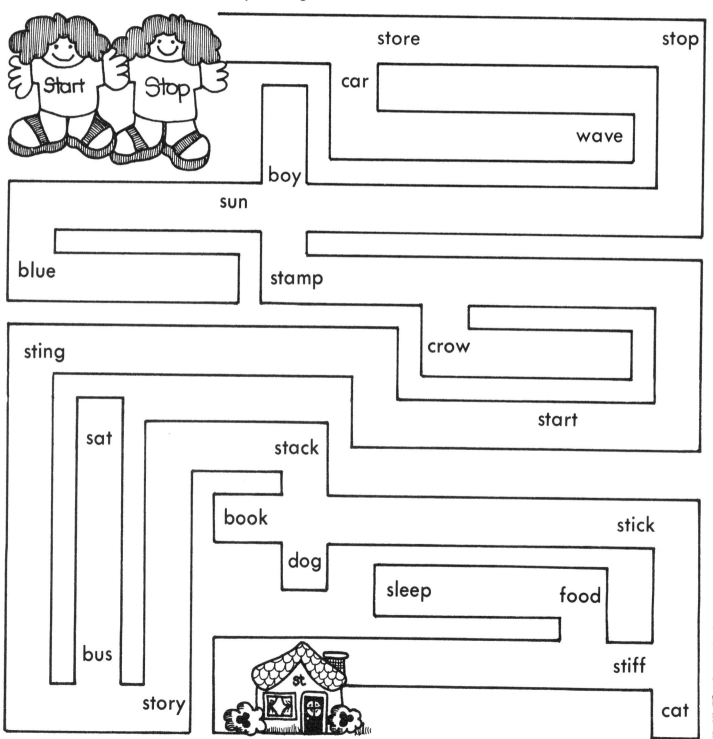

114

st

<u>St</u> can also end words. Then it stands for last.
It is the last sound in last!

Color the words that end in <u>st</u> red.

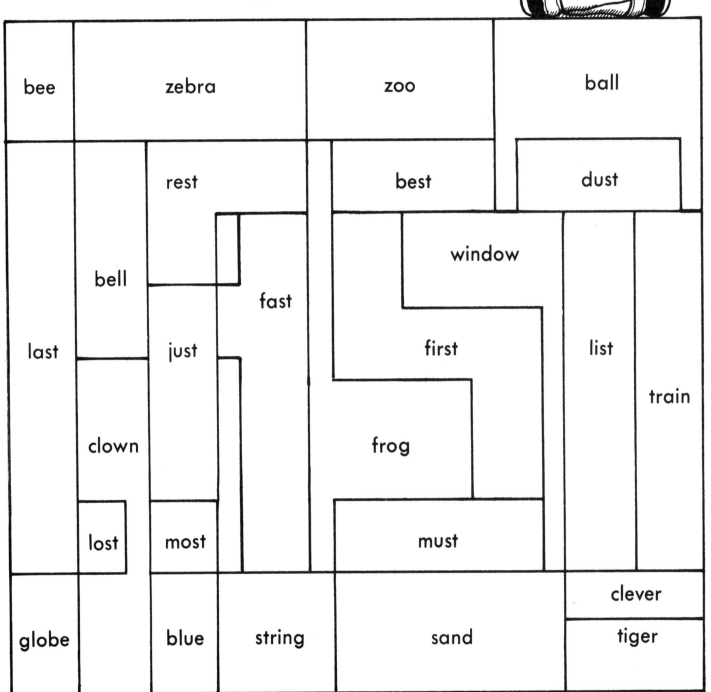

This is NOT the last page!

bee	zebra	zoo	ball
last	rest	best	dust
	bell	window	
	fast	first	list
	just		train
	clown	frog	
	lost	must	
	most		clever
globe	blue string	sand	tiger

The picture says ___ ___ ___ ___.

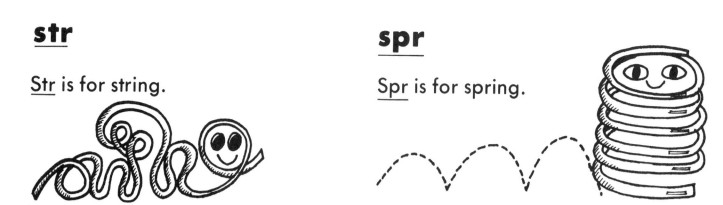

str

Str is for string.

spr

Spr is for spring.

Draw a line around the picture that starts with the blend given.

spr	
spr	
str	
str	
str	

REVIEW: s blends

Look at the picture. Say the picture word. Draw a line around the beginning blend. Write the blend on the blanks. Say the word.

str   **sl**

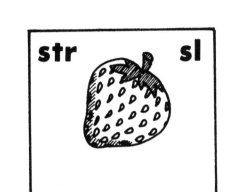

___ ___ ___ awberry

sl   **sn**

___ ___ ail

sm   **st**

___ ___ amp

sp   **str**

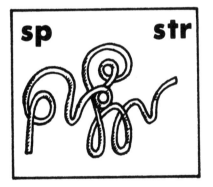

___ ___ ___ ing

st   **sw**

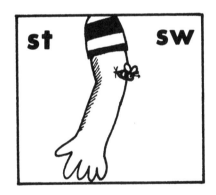

___ ___ ing

st   **sm**

___ ___ ile

sw   **sl**

___ ___ im

sl   **st**

___ ___ op

spr   **st**

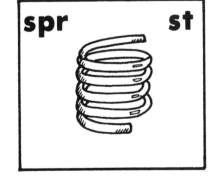

___ ___ ___ ing

117

ch

Ch is for cheese.

Ch is also for porch.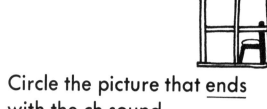

Circle the picture that <u>begins</u> with the <u>ch</u> sound.

Circle the picture that <u>ends</u> with the <u>ch</u> sound.

118

sh

Sh is for sheep.   Sh is also for fish.

Sheep and Fish are all mixed up. They don't know which word belongs to them. Put all the words that start with <u>sh</u> in the sheep pen. Put all the words that end with <u>sh</u> in the fish pond.

ship	shell	dish	shoe	wish
show	shop	wash	shirt	push

th

<u>Th</u> is for thumb.

<u>Th</u> is also for mouth.

Here are some riddles. Put the correct word on the line to answer the riddle.

| bath | south | thing | path | thank | think |

1. "_____ you, Grandma," said Jeff.

2. Karen did not want to take a _____.

3. Birds fly _____ for the winter.

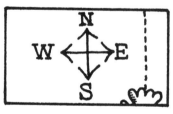

4. I _____ I know the answer.

5. What is this _____?

6. The _____ went into the woods.

wh

Wh is for whale.

Draw a line around the words or the pictures that begin with wh.

wh			
wh	wagon	vase	wheat
wh			
wh	man	woman	why
wh			
wh	green	white	yellow

DIGRAPH REVIEW: <u>ch</u>, <u>sh</u>, <u>th</u>, <u>wh</u>

Draw a line from the letters to the picture words that begin or end with them.

REVIEW

Match the socks to make words. Draw a line from each beginning
sock to each ending sock.

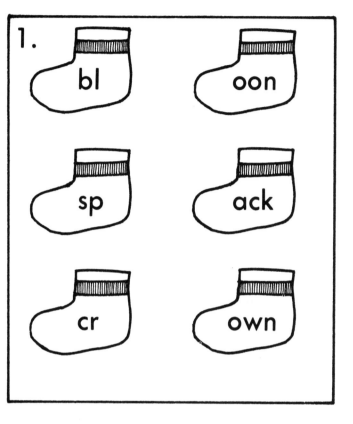

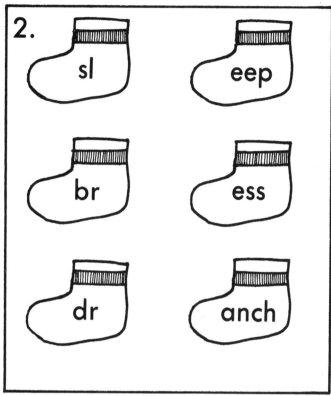

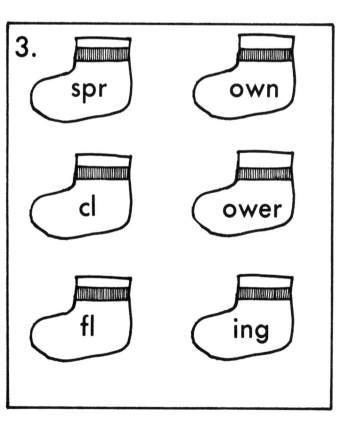

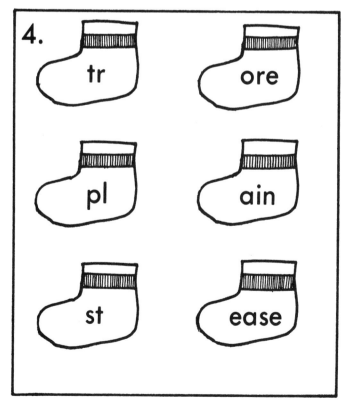

REVIEW

Help the Blue Blender. Make a word for each blend. Write it on the line.

_____   _____

_____   _____

_____   _____

_____   _____

124

DIGRAPHS REVIEW: <u>ch</u>, <u>sh</u>, <u>th</u>, <u>wh</u>

Draw a line from the letters to the picture words that begin with them.

ch

sh

th

wh

REVIEW

Be a worker in the word factory! Make four words in each row. Add the right blend to the last three letters to make a word. Write each word on the line.

bl	br	cl	cr	dr	sl	sm	sn	st	tr

own   **ack**   **ick**

_____   _____   _____

_____   _____   _____

_____   _____   _____

_____   _____   _____

REVIEW

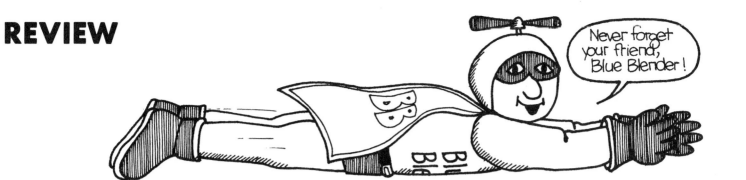

Never forget your friend, Blue Blender!

Read each sentence. Circle the word that starts with the blend given.

pl   1. The girl looked up at the plane.

sn   2. The snail won the race!

pr   3. The prize was a gold cup.

sp   4. Spot had a stick in his mouth.

dr   5. The man drank the water.

gl   6. He drank it from a glass.

sw   7. The cookie was too sweet.

Page 97

Automatic fill in.

Page 98

class climb
clean clock
clown close
clear clever
clay cloud
(clown)

Page 99

Automatic fill in.

Page 100

Automatic fill in.
(glad)

Page 101

1. plan
2. play
3. plant
4. place
5. please

Page 102

sleep
sled
slide
Sleepy Slim

Page 103

1. place
2. blue
3. flag
4. climb
5. sleep

Page 104

1. broom
2. brother
3. brook
4. bright
5. brave
6. branch

Page 105

crown
crow
cross
crib
crayon
cry

Page 106

dress   dream
drop   drink
dragon   dry
drape   drive
(dragon)

Page 107

1. friend
2. front
3. from
4. frog
5. fruits
6. frighten

Page 108

Automatic fill in.

Page 109

(present)
pretty   prison
prize   princess
proud   pray
          present

Page 110

All begin with tr.

Page 116

sprinkler
spring
strawberry
stream
string

Page 111

prize   frog
grass   crow
dragon   tree
bread

Page 112

spider
swim
spoon
swan

Page 113

smoke   smell
snowman   smile
snail   snake

Page 114

store
stop
stamp
start
sting
story
stack
stick
stiff

Page 120

1. thank
2. bath
3. south
4. think
5. thing
6. path

Page 115

last most
rest best
just first
lost must
fast (last)
dust
list

Page 118

church   porch
chair   match
cherries watch

Page 119

ship   dish
shell   wish
shoe   wash
show   push
shop
shirt

Page 121

wheel
wheat
whistle
why
whale
white

Page 117

str sn st
str st sm
sw st spr

Page 126

own   ick
blown   brick
brown   click
clown   slick
crown   stick
drown   trick
ack
black
clack
crack
slack
smack
snack
stack
track

Page 122

ch
match
chair
chicken
sh
sheep
shell
dish
th
teeth or mouth
thumb
path
wh
wheel
whale

Page 123

black   sleep
spoon   branch
crown   dress

spring   train
clown   please
flower   store

Page 124

Any combination:
drag, drink, drove
free, frog
crib, crock
flag, flee, flock
true, trot, tree
snag, snowman
clue, clog, clot, clock
glue, glee, glove
blot, block, blink, blue
spot

Page 125

ch
chicken
church
sh
shoe
ship
th
thumb
thirty
wh
whale
wheel

Page 127

1. plane
2. snail
3. prize
4. spot
5. drank
6. glass
7. sweet

s	l	e	e	p
y	e	s	u	p
b	r	o	w	n
i	s	f	u	n
c	o	w	o	n

Circle the words in the puzzle.
Write the correct word in the blanks.

is   up
yes   fun
brown   cow
on   sleep

1. __ __ __, Amy may leave the room.
2. I want a red one, not a __ __ __ __ __ one.
3. Put the pan __ __ the stove.
4. It is night, and time to go to __ __ __ __ __.
5. What looks like a horse is really a __ __ __.
6. Please don't go __ __ the ladder.
7. Sandy __ __ only two years old.
8. Tom thinks school is __ __ __.

**Circle the words in the puzzle.
Write the correct word in the blanks.**

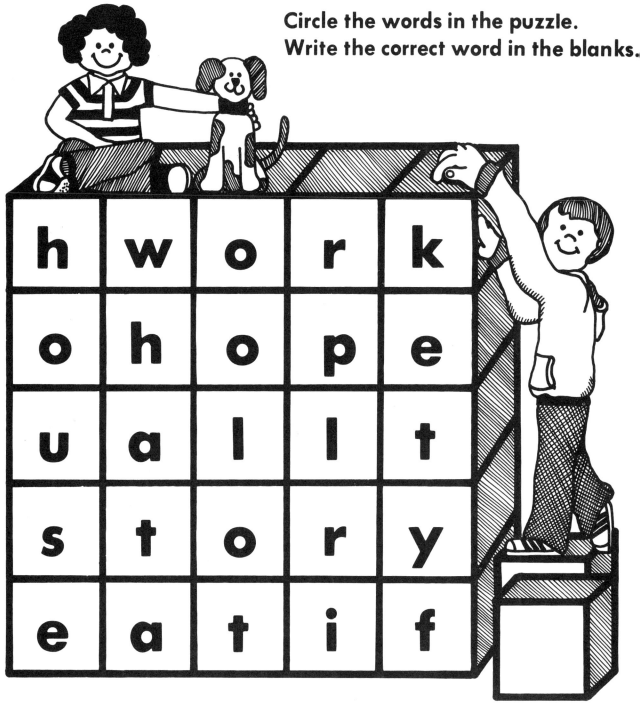

h	w	o	r	k
o	h	o	p	e
u	a	l	l	t
s	t	o	r	y
e	a	t	i	f

all   eat   hope   house
if   story   what   work

1. I __ __ __ __ you get to school on time.
2. Take __ __ __ of the cookies home with you.
3. It is time for Dad to go to __ __ __ __.
4. Be sure to __ __ __ all of your supper.
5. Juan lives in a red and white __ __ __ __ __.
6. Tom won't tell us __ __ he is going or not.
7. Our teacher read us a long __ __ __ __ __.
8. Amy did not know __ __ __ __ to say.

130

WHAT IS IT?

Use the first letter of each picture or the letter given to spell a new word.

bed   candy   coat   dear   eggs   glad   took   well

1. + e + = ___ ___ ___

2. e + + + = ___ ___ ___ ___

3. + o + + = ___ ___ ___ ___

4. + e + + = ___ ___ ___ ___

5. + + + = ___ ___ ___ ___

6. + + + = ___ ___ ___ ___

7. + + + + = ___ ___ ___ ___ ___

8. + + + = ___ ___ ___ ___

Circle the words in the puzzle.

g	r	e	e	n
i	n	d	o	g
r	o	o	m	l
l	i	k	e	s
s	e	e	n	o

in
green
room
see
likes
no
dog
girls

Where is
Brad?

Grass!

Write the correct word in the blanks.

1. Brad put the baby kittens __ __ a box.
2. Sandy has a kitten, but not a __ __ __.
3. He __ __ __ __ __ to ride his bike.
4. The __ __ __ __ has blue walls.
5. The grass is __ __ __ __ __.
6. I don't __ __ __ the airplane in the sky, do you?
7. __ __, you may not have a cookie.
8. They have five __ __ __ __ __ and no boys in their family.

132

Circle the words in the puzzle.

b	l	a	c	k
n	o	w	d	o
i	t	s	o	c
c	a	r	w	d
e	w	a	n	t

its   black
nice   car
now   do
want   down

Write the correct word in the blanks.

1. Go __ __ __ __ the stairs and turn right.
2. Please do the dishes __ __ __.
3. Bob is such a __ __ __ __ friend.
4. There is a __ __ __ __ __ spot on your dress.
5. The bird hurt __ __ __ wing.
6. I will show you how to __ __ it the right way.
7. Buckle your seat belt when you ride in the __ __ __.
8. My brothers __ __ __ __ a train set for Christmas.

Write the correct word in the blanks. Then write the word in the puzzle

bring

girl

kitten

not

playing

think

when

yellow

ACROSS

1. A banana is a __ __ __ __ __ __ fruit.
2. __ __ __ __ __ before you give your answer.
3. Judy is a __ __ __ __.

DOWN

1. Tommy is __ __ __ __ __ __ __ outside today.
2. Father does __ __ __ know what time it is.
3. Sue doesn't know __ __ __ __ they are leaving on vacation.
4. Please __ __ __ __ __ your books when you come.
5. A __ __ __ __ __ __ will grow up to be a cat.

134

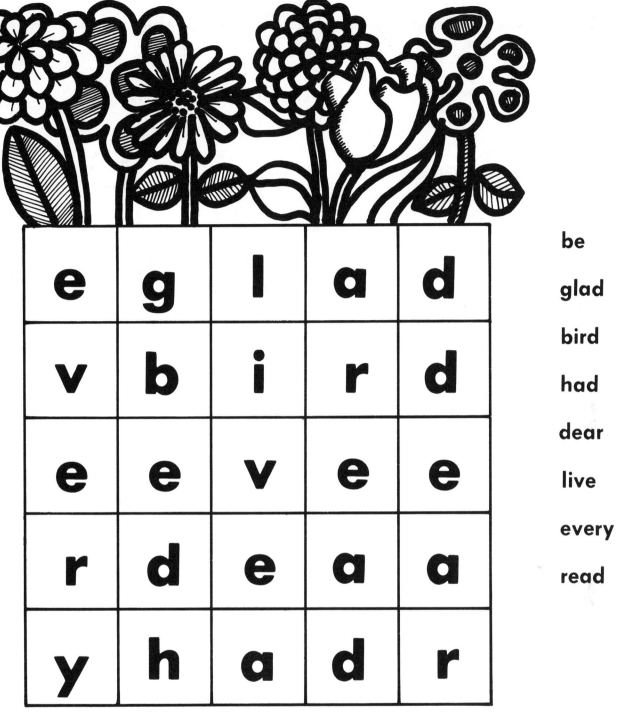

e	g	l	a	d
v	b	i	r	d
e	e	v	e	e
r	d	e	a	a
y	h	a	d	r

be

glad

bird

had

dear

live

every

read

Circle the words in the puzzle.
Write the correct word in the blanks.

1. That __ __ __ __ goes south for the winter.
2. I do not want to __ __ in your way.
3. I am __ __ __ __ to hear that you can come.
4. We can begin a letter by saying, "__ __ __ __ Sir."
5. __ __ __ __ __ child will go to this party.
6. Where does the new girl __ __ __ __?
7. Sue will __ __ __ __ the book to her brother.
8. I __ __ __ a penny, but I lost it.

MISSING VOWELS

Fill in the missing vowels (A,E,I,O and U) for these members of a family.

1. m __ th __ r
2. k __ tt __ n
3. __ __ nt
4. s __ st __ r
5. f __ th __ r
6. d __ g
7. gr __ ndm __
8. gr __ ndp __
9. br __ th __ r
10. __ ncl __

Circle the words in the puzzle. Write the correct word in the blanks.

f	o	u	r	h
r	w	i	l	l
o	h	i	m	i
m	a	n	y	k
I	s	m	a	e

four   from   has   him

I   like   many   will

1. How __ __ __ __ people came to the show?
2. __ will stay with you all the time.
3. Sandy is __ __ __ __ feet tall.
4. Gina __ __ __ __ be the first girl to win.
5. He says he doesn't __ __ __ __ peas.
6. My friend __ __ __ a pet snake.
7. Be sure to let __ __ __ have a turn.
8. Juan is __ __ __ __ the country of Mexico.

Write the correct word in the blanks.
Then write the word in the puzzle.

for   look   father

letter   pet   bear

first   pretty

ACROSS

1. My brother thinks she is a very __ __ __ __ __ __ girl.
2. I wish the mailman would leave me a __ __ __ __ __ __ .
3. That present is __ __ __ Jim.
4. My baby brother said his __ __ __ __ __ word today.

DOWN

1. My dog Spot is my __ __ __ .
2. Before you cross the street, stop, __ __ __ __ , and listen.
3. The man driving the car is my __ __ __ __ __ __ .
4. They say there is a big __ __ __ __ in these woods.

138

g	h	e	l	p
r	a	t	m	b
a	o	o	i	e
d	f	y	l	s
e	f	s	k	t

best
grade
help
milk
off
rat
toys

Circle the words in the puzzle.

Write the correct word in the blanks.

1. Mrs. Van teaches second __ __ __ __ __ in our school.
2. A __ __ __ looks very much like a large mouse.
3. Be sure to put your __ __ __ __ away before going to bed.
4. If you can't do the work alone, ask for __ __ __ __.
5. The __ __ __ __ you drink comes from cows.
6. Please turn __ __ __ the light.
7. Amy is the __ __ __ __ ball player in our whole class.

**Write the correct word in the blanks.
Then write the word in the puzzle.**

apples   did   found   you

boys   tell   old   put

ACROSS

1. My mother uses __ __ __ __ __ __ to make my favorite pie.
2. Your teacher wants to see __ __ __.
3. My grandmother is very __ __ __.
4. Yes, I __ __ __ enjoy my trip.

DOWN

1. Please, __ __ __ your books away.
2. Andy said he wouldn't __ __ __ __ my mother.
3. There are more __ __ __ __ than girls in our class.
4. The lost and __ __ __ __ __ box is in the office.

140

Circle the words in the puzzle.

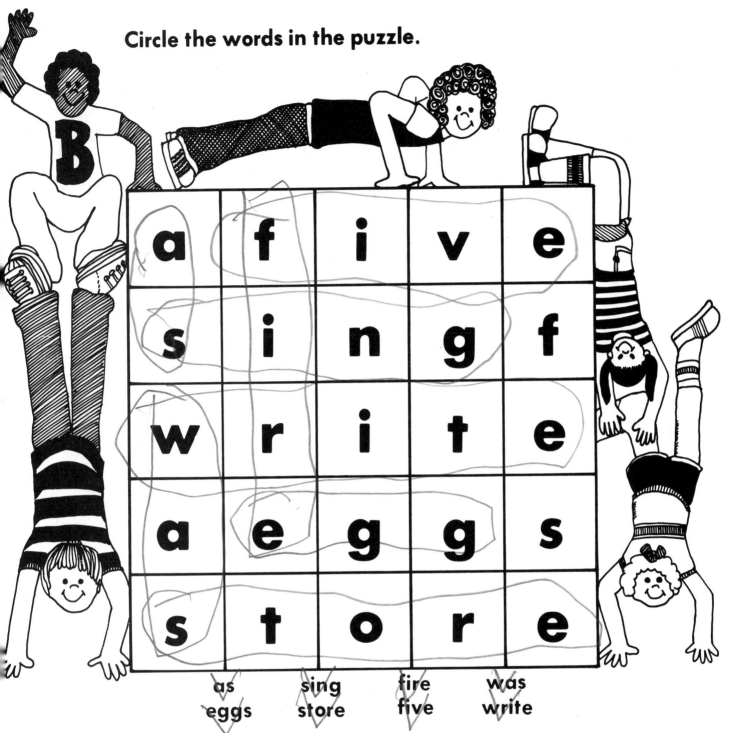

a	f	i	v	e
s	i	n	g	f
w	r	i	t	e
a	e	g	g	s
s	t	o	r	e

as   sing   fire   was

eggs   store   five   write

Write the correct word in the blanks.

1. She wants someone to __ __ __ __ __ her a letter.
2. Tom had four and he wanted __ __ __ __.
3. Mom went to the __ __ __ __ __ for cheese.
4. That bell means there is a __ __ __ __ .
5. He loves to __ __ __ __ that song.
6. Daddy likes __ __ __ __ for breakfast.
7. Grandma __ __ __ sad, but now she is happy.
8. Kim is __ __ tall as I am.

come
dogs
get
made
much
one
school
some

**Write the correct word in the blanks.
Then write the word in the puzzle.**

ACROSS

1. Dad ate too __ __ __ __ for Thanksgiving.
2. We hope Amy will __ __ __ __ to the party.
3. Our baby isn't even __ __ __ year old.
4. I heard a lot of __ __ __ __ barking last night.

DOWN

1. I will take __ __ __ __ of the apples home with me.
2. My sister will go to __ __ __ __ __ __ this year.
3. Sandy __ __ __ __ the dress herself.
4. Do you know what you are going to __ __ __ for Christmas?

142

a	f	t	e	r
t	r	e	e	t
e	y	e	s	a
g	o	t	a	s
d	a	y	w	e

Circle the words in the puzzle.   Write the correct word in the blanks.

1. We are going out to eat __ __ __ __ __ the game.
2. I __ __ __ you run into the house.
3. __ __ will all sing together.
4. Sandy __ __ __ four presents for her birthday.
5. The cat ran up the __ __ __ __.
6. Karen has brown hair and blue __ __ __ __.
7. It is a nice __ __ __ for a walk.
8. Grandpa __ __ __ too much for lunch.

© School Zone Publishing Company

143

an   bed   candy   jump

red   sled   tricks   your

ACROSS

1. Let's teach your dog to do some ___ ___ ___ ___ ___ ___.
2. Too much ___ ___ ___ ___ ___ is bad for your teeth.
3. My dad is out of ___ ___ ___ very early every morning.
4. Don't ___ ___ ___ ___ off the roof! You'll get hurt!

DOWN

1. I would like ___ ___ egg for breakfast.
2. Jane likes her ___ ___ ___ shorts the best.
3. Is that ___ ___ ___ ___ new skateboard?
4. My dog can pull our ___ ___ ___ ___ in the snow.

144

WATCH OUT FOR THE HILL!

c	a	m	e	f
f	i	s	h	g
o	b	h	e	i
o	i	s	o	v
d	g	a	v	e

big   so

came   gave

fish   he

give   food

1. We catch __ __ __ __ in the lake.
2. Tom will __ __ __ __ me a turn next.
3. We eat good __ __ __ __ to stay healthy.
4. Grandma __ __ __ __ to our house on Sunday.
5. She didn't sleep, but __ __ did.
6. I __ __ __ __ Bill a chance to try it.
7. We're late, __ __ hurry up and get dressed.
8. We have a very __ __ __ dog.

YES AND NO

Find the word which means exactly the opposite of the word given. The first one is done for you.

asleep   sit
lost   skinny
she   small
short   stop
sister   yours

1. he   **s h e**

2. tall   s _ _ _ _

3. brother   _ _ s _ _ _

4. start   s _ _ _

5. mine   _ _ _ _ s

6. fat   s _ _ _ _ _

7. stand   s _ _

8. awake   _ s _ _ _ _

9. found   _ _ s _

10. big   s _ _ _ _

146

d	w	i	s	h
r	u	n	h	m
e	t	h	e	a
s	n	o	w	k
s	g	a	m	e

dress   she

game   snow

make   the

run   wish

1. He likes it when she wears her red __ __ __ __ __.
2. Everybody likes __ __ __ __ on Christmas day.
3. Tell Jane __ __ __ may use my skateboard.
4. My grandpa likes to __ __ __ __ things out of wood.
5. We __ __ __ __ you were here with us.
6. Our dog tries to __ __ __ as fast as our car.
7. We are going to the baseball __ __ __ __.
8. He is __ __ __ tallest boy in our class.

Write the correct word in the blanks. Then write the word in the puzzle.

baby
blue
boat
our
play
please
then
wagon

ACROSS

1. Always say __ __ __ __ __ __ and thank-you.
2. My brother is still a __ __ __ __.
3. That red car belongs to __ __ __ family.
4. First we wash, __ __ __ __ we eat.

DOWN

1. When it's raining, you can't __ __ __ __ outside.
2. Kathy went to the lake for a __ __ __ __ ride.
3. My favorite color is __ __ __ __.
4. Molly has a new red __ __ __ __ __.

148

Circle the words in the puzzle.
Write the correct word in the blanks.

a	b	o	u	t
m	a	y	t	a
b	l	u	s	k
e	l	o	v	e
p	a	r	t	y

about   am   ball   love

may   party   take   us

1. I am going to a birthday __ __ __ __ __.
2. Her mother said she __ __ __ go to the beach.
3. I __ __ going to run to the corner.
4. The story is __ __ __ __ __ Jody and her cat.
5. The valentine said, "I __ __ __ __ You."
6. Please __ __ __ __ the dog for a walk.
7. Throw the __ __ __ __ to second base.
8. Those boys want to ride their bikes with __ __.

word bank:
can
horse
ran
second
too
took
water
with

ACROSS

1. Larry is going fishing ___ ___ ___ ___ his dad.
2. He ___ ___ ___ ___ my truck, but he gave it back.
3. Linda likes to ride her ___ ___ ___ ___ ___.
4. Part of a minute is a ___ ___ ___ ___ ___ ___.

DOWN

1. I would like a drink of ___ ___ ___ ___ ___ , please.
2. Wait, I want a ride, ___ ___ ___!
3. Our teacher ___ ___ ___ in a race.
4. Roberto thinks he ___ ___ ___ fix his boat.

150

THE FUNNY WOODS

My mother laughs when I tell her that there are funny things hiding in the woods behind our house. But you and I know better, don't we? Fill in the answer for the clues given, and then circle the "funny thing" in its hiding place.

boots	fish	fork	hat
mouse	pony	train	watch

1. I always wear a __ __ __ on my head in cold weather.
2. A small horse is called a __ __ __ __.
3. A __ __ __ __ __ has an engine, box cars, and a caboose.
4. Use worms when you go to the lake to catch __ __ __ __.
5. Wear __ __ __ __ __ over your shoes when it snows.
6. By my __ __ __ __ __, it's time to leave.
7. Use your __ __ __ __, not your spoon, to eat your meat.
8. A __ __ __ __ __ likes to eat cheese.

Word bank: little, out, over, said, their, very, well, would

ACROSS

1. I __ __ __ __ __ like to go along, but I have to stay here.
2. Sally is too __ __ __ __ __ __ to reach the sink.
3. You should be __ __ __ __ happy today.
4. Bob __ __ __ __ he wouldn't be ready on time.

DOWN

1. Some people get water out of a __ __ __ __ __.
2. The dog ran __ __ __ the door.
3. On our trip we flew __ __ __ __ the ocean.
4. That ball belongs to __ __ __ __ __ school.

152

at   doll   going   last

long   my   new   other

Circle the words in the puzzle.

t	l	o	n	g
d	a	t	e	o
o	s	h	w	i
l	t	e	m	n
l	g	r	y	g

Write the correct word in the blanks.

1. Ed is not __ __ __ __ __ with us today.
2. My sister takes her __ __ __ __ to bed.
3. These pants are too __ __ __ __ for me.
4. What __ __ __ __ __ colors do you have?
5. Tony is __ __ his mother's office.
6. Mr. Andrews is __ __ gym teacher.
7. We need a __ __ __ car.
8. Larry said he would go __ __ __ __ instead of first.

Write the correct word in the blanks.
Then write the word in the puzzle.

back

cold

book

have

by

her

coat

here

ACROSS

1. It is windy and ＿ ＿ ＿ ＿ out today.
2. Dad will be ＿ ＿ ＿ ＿ in an hour.
3. My cousins ＿ ＿ ＿ ＿ six cows in their barn.
4. Jenny says that lady is ＿ ＿ ＿ aunt.

DOWN

1. Grandma is reading a new ＿ ＿ ＿ ＿.
2. Joan is sitting ＿ ＿ the door.
3. I wear a ＿ ＿ ＿ ＿ when it's cold.
4. Come! You can see the mountains from ＿ ＿ ＿ ＿.

154

LET'S TAKE A TRIP

These are things we pack for a trip. What are they?

apple   map

balls   shoes

coat   socks

hat   toothbrush

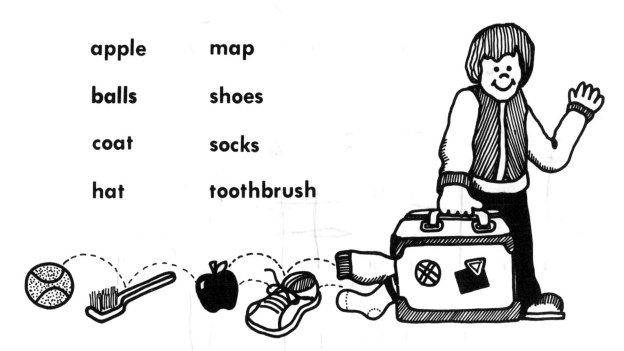

1. You'll need this to keep your teeth clean.
    __ oo __ __ __ __ u __ __
2. You'll wear it to keep your head warm.
    __ a __

3. This __ a __ will help us find our way.

4. You wear them on your feet.
    __ __oe __ and __ o __ __ __

5. I'll need my __ o a __ for cold days.

6. I almost forgot to bring tennis __ a __ __ __.

7. This a __ __ __ e will keep me from getting hungry.

Write the correct word in the blanks. Then write the word in the puzzle.

birds   rabbit   man   mother

his   sister   three   went

ACROSS

1. My dad saw a __ __ __ __ __ __ hop across our yard.
2. That lady over there is my __ __ __ __ __ __.
3. Pedro got hurt and __ __ __ __ home.
4. I have a new baby __ __ __ __ __ __!

DOWN

1. Jon lost __ __ __ bike.
2. My dad is a tall __ __ __.
3. Not all __ __ __ __ __ can fly.
4. Amy is only __ __ __ __ __ years old.

Write the correct word in the blanks.
Then write the word in the puzzle.

go
good
how
morning
soon
them
things
were

ACROSS

1. I don't know __ __ __ to do it.
2. Be sure to eat a good breakfast in the __ __ __ __ __ __ __.
3. Amy wants to __ __ along.
4. We will be leaving for Grandma's house very __ __ __ __.

DOWN

1. I do not want to go with __ __ __ __.
2. How many of your friends __ __ __ __ at the party?
3. Come get your __ __ __ __ __ __ for the trip.
4. My mother makes very __ __ __ __ cookies.

SILLY FARM

Help the animals get to the barn on this Silly Farm. Write the letters in the blanks. The last letter of one word is the first letter of the next word.

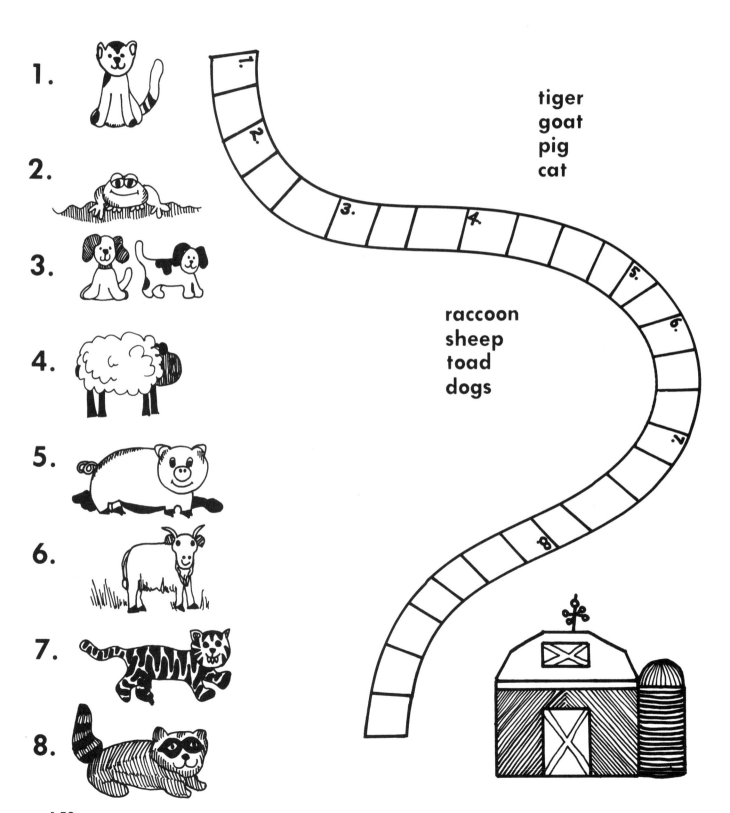

1.

2.

3.

4.

5.

6.

7.

8.

tiger
goat
pig
cat

raccoon
sheep
toad
dogs

ANSWER SHEET GRADE TWO SPELLING

Page 129

1. yes
2. brown
3. on
4. sleep
5. cow
6. up
7. is
8. fun

Page 130

1. hope
2. all
3. work
4. eat
5. house
6. if
7. story
8. what

Page 131

1. bed
2. eggs
3. coat
4. well
5. dear
6. glad
7. candy
8. took

Page 132

1. in
2. dog
3. likes
4. room
5. green
6. see
7. No
8. girls

Page 133

1. down
2. now
3. nice
4. black
5. its
6. do
7. car
8. want

Page 134

ACROSS
1. yellow
2. think
3 girl

DOWN
1. playing
2. not
3. when
4. bring
5. kitten

Page 135

1. bird
2. be
3. glad
4. Dear
5. Every
6. live
7. read
8. had

Page 136

1. mother
2. kitten
3. aunt
4. sister
5. father
6. dog
7. grandma
8. grandpa
9. brother
10. uncle

Page 137

1. many
2. I
3. four
4 will
5. like
6. has
7. him
8. from

Page 138

ACROSS
1 pretty
2 letter
3. for
4. first

DOWN
1. pet
2. look
3. father
4. bear

Page 139

1. grade
2. rat
3. toys
4. help
5. milk
6. off
7. best

Page 140

ACROSS
1. apples
2. you
3. old
4. did

DOWN
1. put
2. tell
3. boys
4. found

Page 141

1. write
2. five
3. store
4. fire
5. sing
6. eggs
7. was
8. as

Page 142

ACROSS
1. much
2. come
3. one
4. dogs

DOWN
1. some
2. school
3. made
4. get

Page 143

1. after
2. saw
3. We
4. got
5. tree
6. eyes
7. day
8. ate

Page 144

ACROSS
1. tricks
2. candy
3. bed
4. jump

DOWN
1. an
2. red
3. your
4. sled

Page 145

1. fish
2. give
3. food
4. came
5. he
6. gave
7. so
8. big

Page 146

1. she
2. short
3. sister
4. stop
5. yours
6. skinny
7. sit
8. asleep
9. lost
10. small

Page 147

1. dress
2. snow
3. she
4. make
5. wish
6. run
7. game
8. the

Page 148

ACROSS
1. please
2. baby
3. our
4. then

DOWN
1. play
2. boat
3. blue
4. wagon

Page 149

1. party
2. may
3. am
4. about
5. Love
6. take
7. ball
8. us

Page 150

ACROSS
1. with
2. took
3. horse
4. second

DOWN
1. water
2. too
3. ran
4. can

Page 151

1. hat
2. pony
3. train
4. fish
5. boots
6. watch
7. fork
8. mouse

Page 152

ACROSS
1. would
2. little
3. very
4. said

DOWN
1. well
2. out
3. over
4. their

Page 153

1. going
2. doll
3. long
4. other
5. at
6. my
7. new
8. last

Page 154

ACROSS
1. cold
2. back
3. have
4. her

DOWN
1. book
2. by
3. coat
4. here

Page 155

1. toothbrush
2. hat
3. map
4. shoes socks
5. coat
6. balls
7. apple

Page 156

ACROSS
1. rabbit
2. mother
3. went
4. sister

DOWN
1. his
2. man
3. birds
4. three

Page 157

ACROSS
1. how
2. morning
3. go
4. soon

DOWN
1. them
2. were
3. things
4. good

Page 158

1. cat
2. toad
3. dogs
4. sheep
5. pig
6. goat
7. tiger
8. raccoon

160

Read each sentence.
Circle the picture that goes with it.

The dog has a birthday.

Dad paints the house.

Here comes the train.

Mother jumps.

Cold Cat rides a bike.

I see two fish.

This car is little.

Read each sentence.
Circle the picture that goes with it.

See the big boat.

We like to run.

The bird is wet.

Cold Cat plays ball.

The goat ate a hat.

Thank you for the book.

They are happy.

Circle the correct word for each sentence.

Amy is my (**brother**   **sister**).

I have a red (**dress**   **hat**).

Stop that (**bus**   **car**).

There is (**word**   **water**) in the wagon.

We must (**hide**   **help**) Cold Cat.

Give the (**did**   **dog**) some water.

Let's go to the (**zoo**   **zebra**).

Circle the correct word for each sentence.

The (**duck** **dark**) can swim.

I hear the dog (**book** **bark**).

We like to eat (**food** **from**).

See the (**moon** **make**) in the sky.

Look at the (**dish** **dress**).

The girl rides a (**house** **horse**).

Cold Cat likes to (**soon** **sleep**).

Draw a line from each sentence to the correct picture.

It lives in the water.

This is big and yellow.

It can fly.

This animal is cold.

You can ride on this.

This animal is wet.

You can sleep in it.

Draw a line from each sentence to the correct picture.

There are four of these.

Children go here.

It lives in a barn.

Please do not cry.

There are five of these.

It lives in a nest.

It has two very big feet.

Read each sentence.
Do what it says.

Color Cold Cat **orange**.

Color his cap **purple**.

Color the dog **black** and the car **red**.

Color the house **yellow**.

Color the pig **pink** and her coat **green**.

Read each sentence.
Do what it says.

Write **1** next to the rabbit.

Write **2** next to the horse.

Write **3** next to the rocket.

Draw an **O** around the men.

Write **C** on Cold Cat.

Write **X** on the box.

Draw a ✔ on the balloon.

168

Circle **Yes** if the sentence is true.
Circle **No** if it is not true.

Yes	**No**	You can eat a boot.
Yes	**No**	Cold Cat can bark.
Yes	**No**	A book will bite.
Yes	**No**	**Three** comes after **two**.
Yes	**No**	A mouse is small.
Yes	**No**	Elephants are green.
Yes	**No**	**Four** comes before **five**.
Yes	**No**	A kitten is a baby cat.

Circle **Yes** if the sentence is true.
Circle **No** if it is not true.

(Yes)	No	Snow is white.
(Yes)	No	It is dark at night.
Yes	(No)	A penny is not round.
(Yes)	No	Cars go on streets.
(Yes)	No	A boy can walk up a hill.
(Yes)	No	A girl can walk down a hill.
Yes	(No)	Fire is cold.
Yes	(No)	Cold Cat has a tail.

Words that rhyme have the same last sound.
Who, **zoo**, **blue**, and **you** all rhyme.
Read each sentence.
Write the word that **rhymes** with the bold word on each line.

sun   sat   big   you   fan   train   red

The **man** holds a __fan__.

Did it **rain** on the _____?

Bob will **run** in the _____.

Who will give the ball to _____?

Lee will paint the **bed** _____.

Cold **Cat** _____.

That **pig** is very _____.

Read each sentence.
Write the word that **rhymes** with the bold word on each line.

pie   away   cake   too   dish   tree   book

Will you go _____ to **play**?

Stop! Don't you **see** the _____?

Cold Cat **took** the _____.

This is **my** apple _____.

Please **take** the _____.

The **fish** jumped out of the _____!

This hat is _____ **blue**.

Circle the sentence that goes with each picture.

Run up the hill!
Here we go down the hill.

That duck has three boots.
That duck has four boots.

Two birds sit in a cage.
Two birds sit on a cow.

I read at school.
I read at home.

Cold Cat sits by the fire.
Cold Cat puts out the fire.

Stop that horse!
Help that horse!

Circle the sentence that goes with each picture.

This bear is too small.
This bear is too big.

Cold Cat will fly the plane.
Cold Cat will ride the train.

Where are my boots?
Where are my mittens?

The coat is on the boy.
The goat is in the pen.

The baby is on the box.
The box is on the baby.

The pony and pig race.
The pony wins.

174

Circle the sentence that goes with each picture.

It is morning!
Please go to sleep.

Say hello to the duck.
Say goodbye to the bird.

My friend lives on a farm.
My friend plays a game with me.

Cold Cat has five feet.
Cold Cat sings a song.

I see three toy trucks.
I see three toy cars.

Amy hurt her leg.
Amy helps her mother.

Look at each picture and sentence.
Write the correct word on the line.

truck   ice   baby   light   pan   walks   three

The ___baby___ sleeps.

The _____ is very clean.

Two eggs are in the _____ .

Please turn off the _____ .

Cold Cat is happy when he _____ .

We like to skate on _____ .

Ann has _____ brothers.

176

Look at each picture and sentence.
Write the correct word on the line.

turtle Five name cut behind Children pocket

He will _____ the cake.

The dog is _____ the big tree.

_____ like to play.

Your mittens are in your _____ .

_____ ducks fly away.

My _____ is Jim.

Cold Cat finds a _____ .

Look at each picture and sentence.
Write the correct word on the line.

four   hair   under   girl   hold   letter   party

The _____ gave me a picture.

This _____ is for me!

Ms. SQUIRREL
2 TREE WAY
GROVE, PINE
NUTS

Please _____ this box for me.

Cold Cat is _____ the bed.

_____ men were in the water.

Jenny has a birthday _____ .

Her _____ is very long.

178

Draw a line from each sentence to the answer.

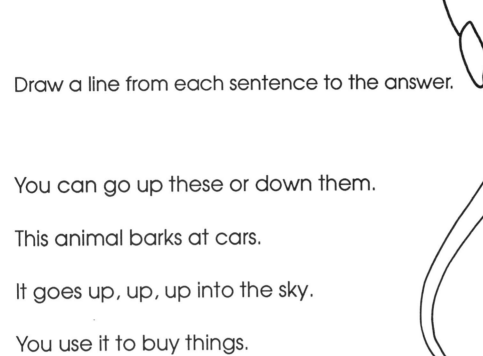

You can go up these or down them.   **clock**

This animal barks at cars.   **mouse**

It goes up, up, up into the sky.   **money**

You use it to buy things.   **steps**

It is a very small animal.   **dog**

You say **Hello** on it.   **rocket**

It tells you the time.   **phone**

Draw a line from each sentence to the answer.

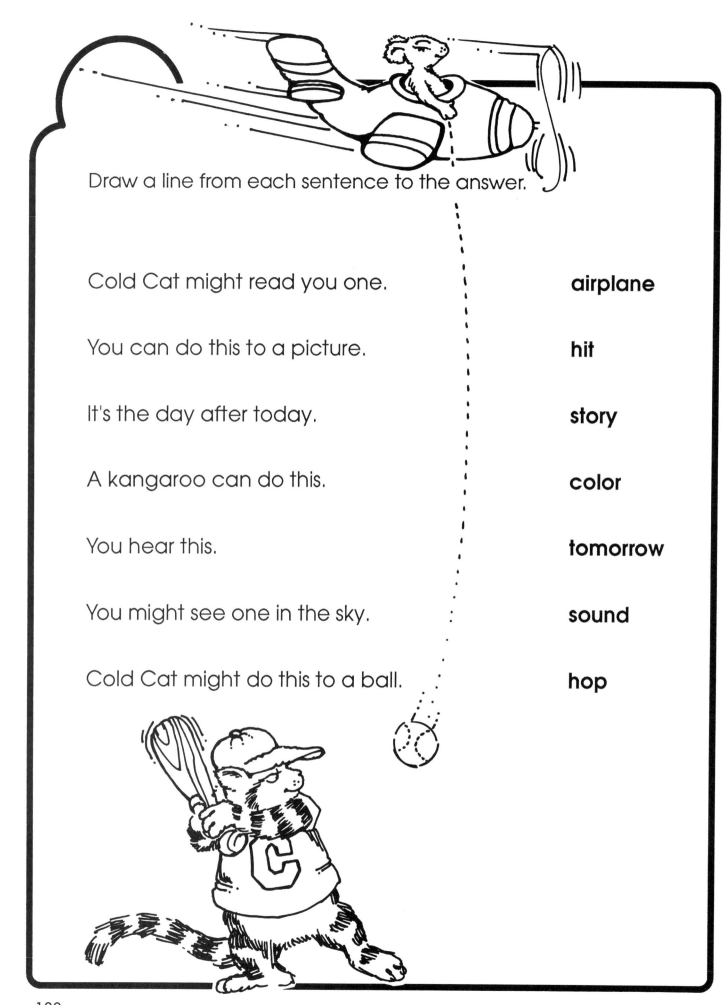

Cold Cat might read you one.   **airplane**

You can do this to a picture.   **hit**

It's the day after today.   **story**

A kangaroo can do this.   **color**

You hear this.   **tomorrow**

You might see one in the sky.   **sound**

Cold Cat might do this to a ball.   **hop**

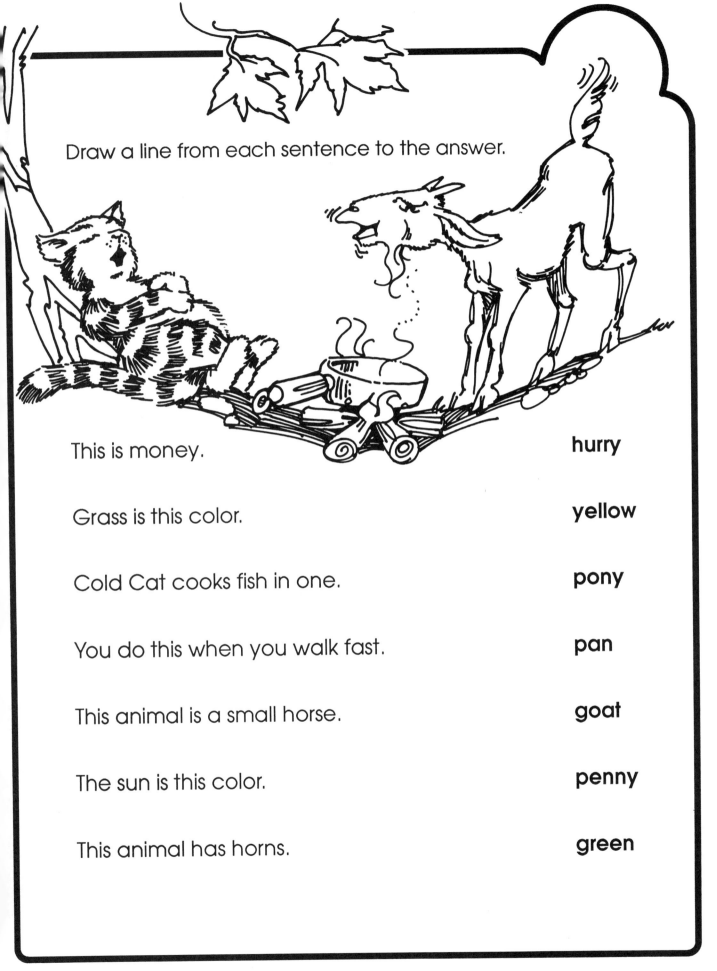

Draw a line from each sentence to the answer.

This is money.   **hurry**

Grass is this color.   **yellow**

Cold Cat cooks fish in one.   **pony**

You do this when you walk fast.   **pan**

This animal is a small horse.   **goat**

The sun is this color.   **penny**

This animal has horns.   **green**

Read each sentence.
Do what it says.

Two birds are the same. **Circle** them.

Two birds are different. Draw a **box** around them.

Color Cold Cat **yellow**.

Color the mouse **red**.

Write **L** next to the long snake.

Write **S** next to the short snake.

Draw a **box** around Cold Cat and the mouse.

Read each sentence.
Do what it says.

Draw an **X** by the real Cold Cat.

Draw a big **C** on his shirt.

Draw a **happy face** on the girl.

Draw a **sad face** on the boy.

Two caps are the same. Draw a **box** around them.

Two caps are different. Draw a **circle** around them.

Which duck is bigger? Color it **green** and **brown**.

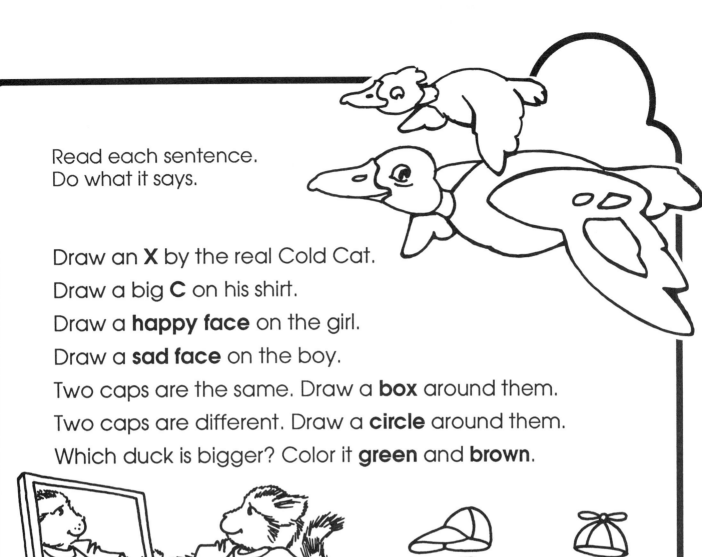

Read each sentence.
Do what it says.

Draw a **line** under the wagon.

Draw **two lines** over the dragon.

Draw **two circles** around Cold Cat.

Write **L** on Cold Cat's left hand.

Write **R** on Cold Cat's right hand.

Two mittens go together. Color them **red** and **blue.**

Two mittens do not go together. Draw a **box** around them.

184

Circle **Yes** if the sentence is true.
Circle **No** if it is not true.

Yes   **No**   Two boots can sing a song.

Yes   **No**   A cat might be cold.

Yes   **No**   Rabbits can hop.

Yes   **No**   A brother is a girl.

Yes   **No**   A big yellow bus has four feet.

Yes   **No**   Children can go to school.

Yes   **No**   **Six** comes after **ten**.

Yes   **No**   Fire trucks eat fish.

Circle **Yes** if the sentence is true.
Circle **No** if it is not true.

Yes	**No**	A **mother** is a **mom**.
Yes	**No**	You can look out of a window.
Yes	**No**	There are no animals in a zoo.
Yes	**No**	You can carry things in a basket.
Yes	**No**	A penny is something to wear.
Yes	**No**	**D** comes after **C**.
Yes	**No**	A cat can have kittens.
Yes	**No**	A cupcake is something to eat.

Circle **Yes** if the sentence is true.
Circle **No** if it is not true.

Yes	**No**	All elephants are very little.
Yes	**No**	Apples and cookies are food.
Yes	**No**	A box is always round.
Yes	**No**	You can buy eggs in a store.
Yes	**No**	A cat has four tails.
Yes	**No**	**Stop** is not the same as **go**.
Yes	**No**	**Four** comes before **five**.
Yes	**No**	A book is something to read.

Read the first sentence in each group.
Then read the next two sentences.
Write an **X** next to the one that **rhymes** with the first sentence.

Cold Cat stops the train.

_____ Cold Cat has no car.

__X__ Cold Cat has no brain.

Cold Cat goes to bed.

_____ Cold Cat hides his head.

_____ Cold Cat says good night.

Mother, Mother, take my book.

_____ Put it on the table.

_____ Put it in the pot to cook.

Cold Cat paints a sled.

_____ Every day he paints it black.

_____ Every day he paints it red.

Read the first sentence in each group.
Then read the next two sentences.
Write an **X** next to the one that **rhymes** with the first sentence.

Cold Cat paints his shoe.

_____ Cold Cat paints it blue.

_____ Cold Cat paints it green.

Linda saw the box and made a guess.

_____ In the box was a glass.

_____ In the box was a dress.

Mom can cook and Mom can bake.

_____ Mom gives me a big cupcake.

_____ Mom gives me a good cookie.

In the chair sat a dog.

_____ On the ground sat a cat.

_____ On the ground sat a frog.

Read the first sentence in each group.
Then read the next two sentences.
Write an **X** next to the one that **rhymes** with the first sentence.

Listen to what Grandma said.

_____ Never paint a tiger red.

_____ Never paint a tiger green.

Cold Cat finds some money.

_____ Cold Cat buys a mouse.

_____ Cold Cat thinks it's funny.

I see something in a chair.

_____ Can it be a cat?

_____ Can it be a bear?

What a very funny pen.

_____ I will give it to the hen.

_____ I will give it to the man.

Color the picture.
Then write a story about Cold Cat.

_____

_____

_____

_____

_____

_____

191

ANSWER KEY

Page 163
sister
dress
bus
water
help
dog
zoo

Page 164
duck
bark
food
moon
dish
horse
sleep

Page 169
No
No
No
Yes
Yes
No
Yes
Yes

Page 170
Yes
Yes
No
Yes
Yes
Yes
No
Yes

Page 171
fan
train
sun
you
red
sat
big

Page 172
away
tree
book
pie
cake
dish
too

Page 173
Run up the hill!
That duck has four boots.
Two birds sit on a cow.
I read at home.
Cold Cat sits by the fire.
Stop that horse!

Page 174
This bear is too big.
Cold Cat will ride the train.
Where are my boots?
The goat is in the pen.
The baby is on the box.
The pony wins.

Page 175
It is morning!
Say goodbye to the bird.
My friend plays a game with me.
Cold Cat sings a song.
I see three toy cars.
Amy hurt her leg.

Page 176
baby
truck
pan
light
walks
ice
three

Page 177
cut
behind
Children
pocket
Five
name
turtle

Page 178
girl
letter
hold
under
Four
party
hair

Page 179
steps
dog
rocket
money
mouse
phone
clock

Page 180
story
color
tomorrow
hop
sound
airplane
hit

Page 181
penny
green
pan
hurry
pony
yellow
goat

Page 185
No
Yes
Yes
No
No
Yes
No
No

Page 186
Yes
Yes
No
Yes
No
Yes
Yes
Yes

Page 187
No
Yes
No
Yes
No
Yes
Yes
Yes

Page 188
Cold Cat has no brain.
Cold Cat hides his head.
Put it in the pot to cook.
Every day he paints it red.

Page 189
Cold Cat paints it blue.
In the box was a dress.
Mom gives me a big cupcake.
On the ground sat a frog.

Page 190
Never paint a tiger red.
Cold Cat thinks it's funny.
Can it be a bear?
I will give it to the hen.

192

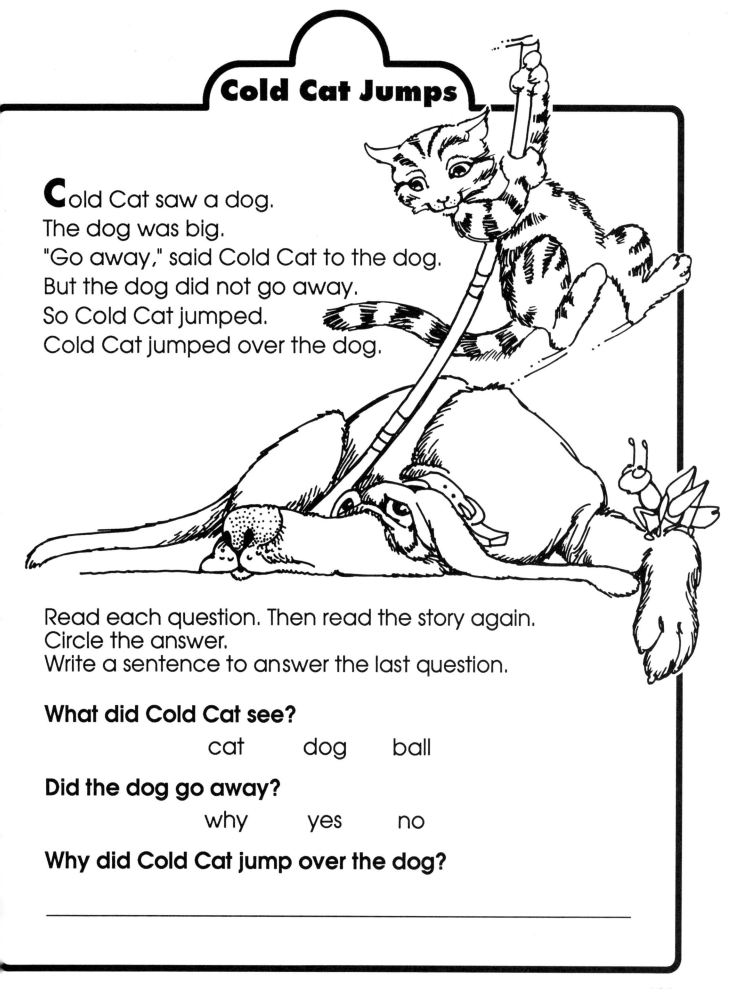

Cold Cat Jumps

Cold Cat saw a dog.
The dog was big.
"Go away," said Cold Cat to the dog.
But the dog did not go away.
So Cold Cat jumped.
Cold Cat jumped over the dog.

Read each question. Then read the story again.
Circle the answer.
Write a sentence to answer the last question.

What did Cold Cat see?

                 cat   dog   ball

Did the dog go away?

                 why   yes   no

Why did Cold Cat jump over the dog?

_____

The Red Cake

Scott likes cars. And Scott likes the color red.

It is Scott's birthday.
Scott gets a big cake.
The cake looks like a car! It looks like a big red car.

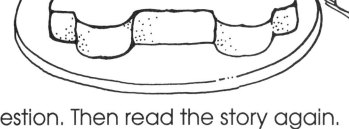

Read each question. Then read the story again.
Circle the answer.
Write a sentence to answer the last question.

What does Scott like?

        trucks   cakes   cars

What color does Scott like?

        blue   red   yellow

What does the cake look like?

_____

The big dog got up. Then the big dog ran after Cold Cat.

Cold Cat ran away.

"Help!" said Cold Cat.

Cold Cat saw a house. Cold Cat ran into the house. Then Cold Cat locked the door.

Read the sentences below. Then read the story again. Number the sentences in story order. Number them **1**, **2**, **3**, and **4**.

_____   **The big dog ran after Cold Cat.**

_____   **Cold Cat locked the door.**

_____   **Cold Cat ran into the house.**

_____   **The big dog got up.**

Ann has a pet goat. The name of her goat is Bit.

Bit likes to eat. One day he ate the dog's food.

One day he ate Ann's cake.

Bit likes to eat grass, too. Ann likes it when Bit eats grass.

Read each question. Then read the story again.
Circle the answer.
Write a sentence to answer the last question.

Who is Bit?

goat   dog   cake

What does Bit like to do?

run   play   eat

Why does Ann like it when Bit eats grass?

_____

Hello, Dog

Cold Cat looked at the dog.

"Hello," said the dog. "My name is Hot Dog. I am always hot."

"Hello," said Cold Cat. "My name is Cold Cat. I am always cold."

"Come out and play," said Hot Dog.

So that is what Cold Cat did.

Read each question. Then read the story again.
Circle the answer.
Write a sentence to answer the last question.

Who said "Hello" first?

               cat   dog   bird

Who is always hot?

              dog   goat   cat

Why is Cold Cat called Cold Cat?

_____

Who Took My Book?

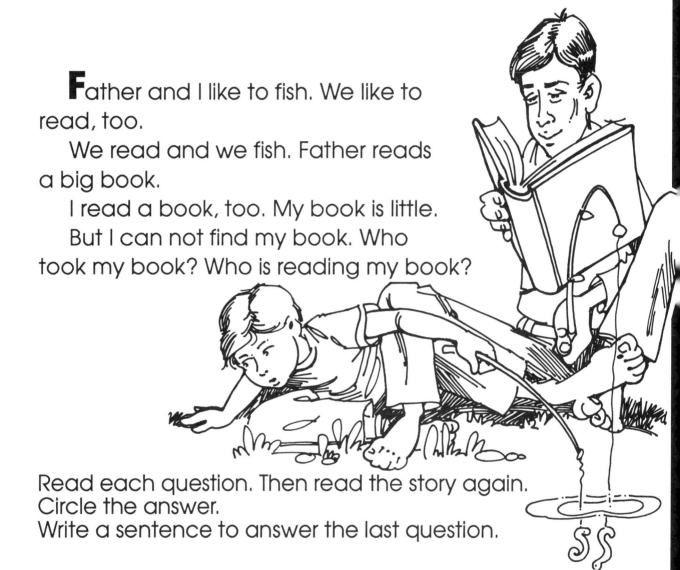

Father and I like to fish. We like to read, too.

We read and we fish. Father reads a big book.

I read a book, too. My book is little.

But I can not find my book. Who took my book? Who is reading my book?

Read each question. Then read the story again.
Circle the answer.
Write a sentence to answer the last question.

Who reads a big book?

        boy   fish   father

Who can not find his book?

        boy   father   fish

Who reads the little book now?

_____

198

The First Pink Pig

Once there were three pink pigs.
The first pink pig said, "I will make a house."

"I will make a pink house," she said. "I will make my house out of balloons."

So the first pink pig made a house. She made it out of pink balloons. She was very happy.

Read the words. Then read the story again.
Write each word on the correct line.

first   **balloon**   **pink**

This is a color. It is _____.

This comes before the second. It comes _____.

This is a toy. It is a _____.

Cold Kitten

"I am a cold cat," said the little cat.

"No," said Cold Cat. "You are Cold Kitten. When you are little, you are a kitten."

Cold Kitten saw two dogs. One was big and one was little. "There is a dog and a kitten," said Cold Kitten.

"No, no!" said Cold Cat. "A little dog is a puppy. Only a little cat is a kitten."

Read the words. Then read the story again. Write each word on the correct line.

puppy   kitten   little

A little cat is a _____.

A kitten is _____.

A little dog is a _____.

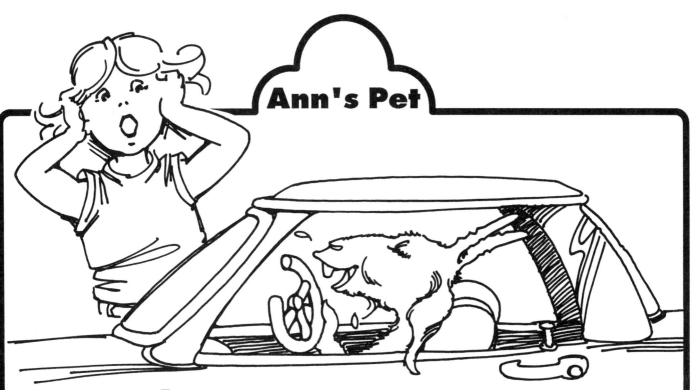

Ann's Pet

Ann has a pet. The pet's name is Bit. Ann could not find her pet. She looked in the yard. But Bit was not in the yard.

So Ann looked in the house. Bit was not in the house.

Then Ann looked in the car. There was Bit! Bit was in the car.

Read the sentences below. Then read the story again.
Number the sentences in story order.
Number them **1**, **2**, **3**, and **4**.

_____ **She found Bit in the car.**

_____ **Ann looked in the yard.**

_____ **She looked in the house.**

_____ **Ann could not find her pet.**

Cold Kitten saw a little goat. "There is a puppy," she said.

"No, no!" said Cold Cat. "There is a kid, not a puppy. A little goat is called a kid."

Cold Kitten saw a boy. "There is a kid," she said.

"Yes," said Cold Cat. "There is a kid."

Read each question. Then read the story again.
Circle the answer.
Write a sentence to answer the last question.

What is a little goat called?

puppy   kitten   kid

Who did Cold Kitten talk to?

Hot Dog   Cold Cat   Big Boy

What is a boy or girl called?

_____

How to Feed Your Dog

Do you have a dog? Then you must feed your dog. Here is how.

First find the dog dish. Put the dish down.

Then get the bag of dog food. Put some dog food in the dish.

Now move away! Let your dog eat!

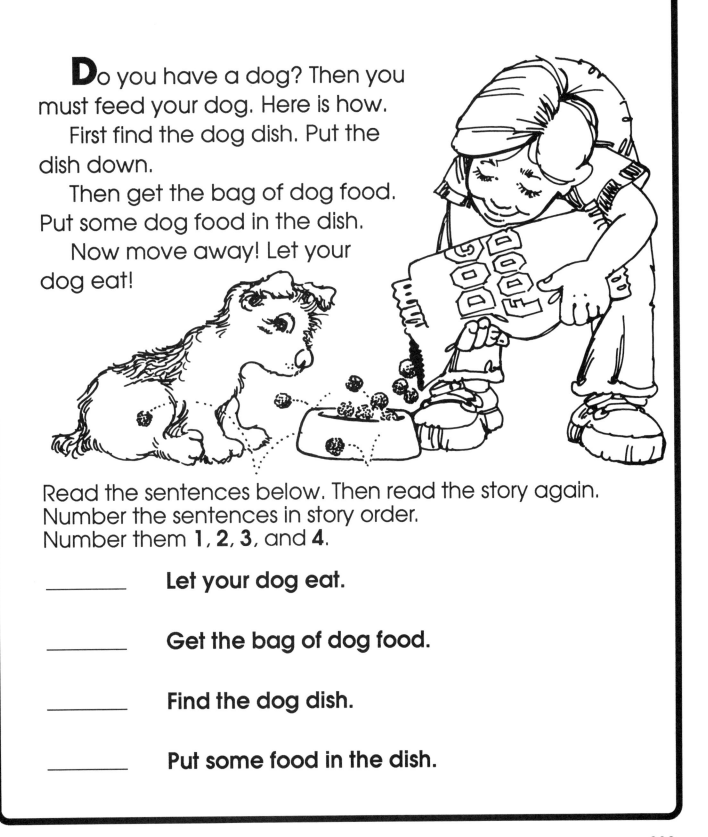

Read the sentences below. Then read the story again.
Number the sentences in story order.
Number them **1, 2, 3,** and **4**.

_____ **Let your dog eat.**

_____ **Get the bag of dog food.**

_____ **Find the dog dish.**

_____ **Put some food in the dish.**

The Second Pink Pig

The first pink pig made a house. She made it out of pink balloons.

The second pink pig looked at the balloons. The second pink pig said, "I will make a house, too. I will make a pink house."

So the second pink pig made a house. She made it out of pink gum.

"There," said the second pink pig. "A gum house is better."

GUM

Read the sentences below. Then read the story again. Number the sentences in story order. Number them **1**, **2**, **3**, and **4**.

_____ **The first pink pig made a balloon house.**

_____ **The second pig said, "A gum house is better."**

_____ **The second pig made a pink gum house.**

_____ **The second pig looked at the balloon house.**

Up, Up, Up

Hot Dog runs after Cold Cat. Cold Cat runs very fast. But Hot Dog runs faster.

Cold Cat sees a tree. Cold Cat goes up the tree. Up, up, up!

Hot Dog cannot go up a tree. Hot Dog is down.

Cold Cat laughs at Hot Dog.

Read each question.
Then read the story again.
Circle the answer.

Who runs faster?

Cold Cat   tree   Hot Dog

Who is up?

faster   Cold Cat   Hot Dog

Who is down?

Hot Dog   Cold Cat   tree

Why does Cold Cat laugh?

_____

The Goat in the Coat

The goat put on a coat. Then the goat went out.

A wolf looked at the goat. "You are a big goat," said the wolf. "I will not run after you."

The goat went to the store. The goat got a hat.

Then the goat went home. The goat took off the coat. It was a big, big coat. The coat was big, but the goat was not.

Read each question. Then read the story again. Circle the answer.

Who would not run after the goat?

coat   wolf   store

Where did the goat go?

store   school   up

What did the goat buy?

coat   wolf   hat

Why did the goat have on a big, big coat?

_____

The Third Pink Pig

"I will make a house," said the third pink pig. "I will make a pink house. It will be the best pink house."

So the third pink pig got in her truck. She took the truck to town. Then she came back. She came back with many bricks.

The third pink pig made a house. She made her house out of pink bricks.

Read the words. Then read the story again.
Write each word on the correct line.

truck   third   bricks

It was not first or second, but _____.

You can build with _____.

A _____ is like a car but bigger.

At the Zoo

Mom took Jason and Sara to the zoo.

Jason wanted to see the tigers.
So they all went to see the tigers.
Sara wanted to see the bears.
So they all went to see the bears.
Mom wanted to see the zebras.
So they all went to see the zebras.
Then they all went home.

Read the words. Then read the story again.
Write each word on the correct line.

tigers   zoo   home

The place where you live is your _____.

Big cats that are orange and black are _____.

You can see animals at the _____.

Hot Dog

Hot Dog was hot. Yes, hot!
"I do not want to be hot," said
Hot Dog. "I want to be cold."

Hot Dog got a box. Then he got
cold water. He put the cold water
in the box.

Hot Dog sat in the box of cold
water. At last, Hot Dog was not hot.

Read each question. Then read the story again.
Write a sentence to answer each question.

What did Hot Dog do first?

_____

What did Hot Dog do second?

_____

Why was Hot Dog not hot at last?

_____

Show and Tell

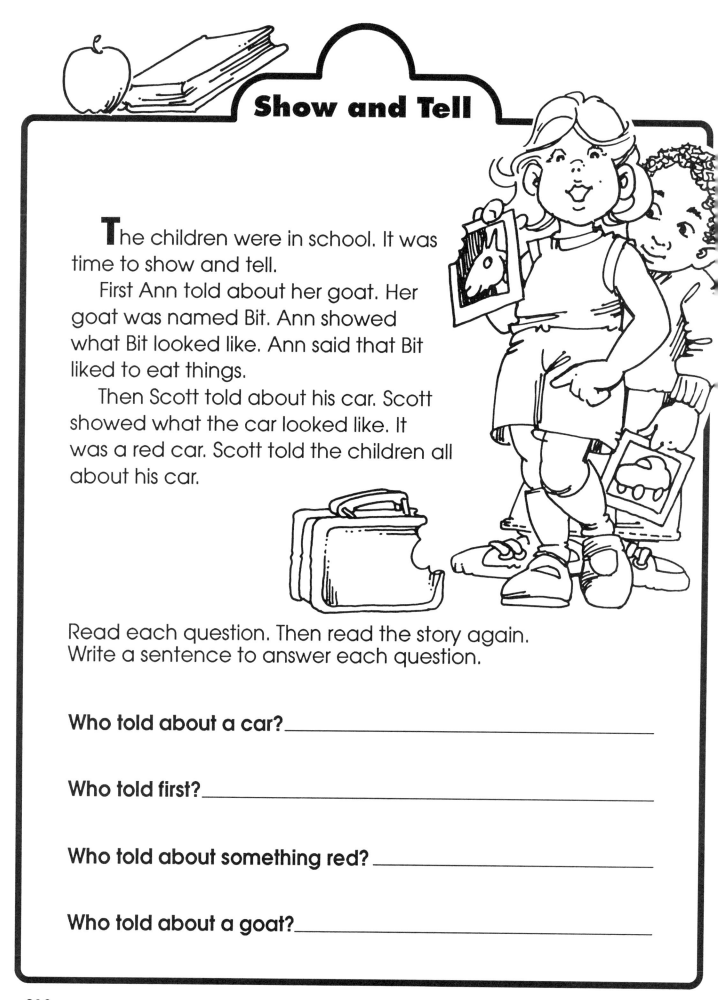

The children were in school. It was time to show and tell.

First Ann told about her goat. Her goat was named Bit. Ann showed what Bit looked like. Ann said that Bit liked to eat things.

Then Scott told about his car. Scott showed what the car looked like. It was a red car. Scott told the children all about his car.

Read each question. Then read the story again. Write a sentence to answer each question.

Who told about a car?_____

Who told first?_____

Who told about something red? _____

Who told about a goat?_____

210

Which Is Best?

The three pink pigs looked. They looked at the three houses.

"My house is best," said the first pink pig. "My house is best because it is made of pink balloons."

"No," said the second pink pig. "My house is best. It is best because it is made of pink gum."

The third pink pig said, "No, my house is best. It is best because it is made of pink bricks."

This story is called **Which Is Best?**
Which Is Best? helps tell what the story is about.
Circle two other titles that help tell what the story is about.

The Three Pink Pigs   **A Day at School**

The Big Bad Wolf   **Three Pink Houses**

Write your own title for this story.

_____

Walking to Town

Cold Cat and Cold Kitten walked to town.

As they walked, rain came down. Down, down, down.

"We are walking in the rain," said Cold Kitten.

"Yes," said Cold Cat. "We are walking in the rain. But we are not wet."

This story is called **Walking to Town**.
Walking to Town helps tell what the story is about.
Circle two other titles that help tell what the story is about.

Cold Cat Goes Home   **We Are Not Wet**

Walking in the Rain   **Cold Kitten Is Hot**

212

Give Me Boots

"I need boots," said Sara. "I do not want my feet to get wet."

Jason said, "I need boots, too. I want yellow boots for the rain."

So Dad took Jason and Sara to the store. "You will get rain boots," said Dad. "And you will get snow boots, too."

Sara got red boots and blue boots.

Jason got yellow boots and green boots.

Read each question. Then read the story again.
Write a sentence to answer each question.

What did Sara need for her feet?

_____

What color boots did Jason want?

_____

Why did Dad buy Sara and Jason both rain boots and snow boots?

_____

The Big Sad Wolf

"My house is best," said the first pink pig. "No, mine is best," said the second pink pig. "No, my house is best," the third pink pig said.

Just then, the three pigs saw a wolf. He was a big wolf. He was a sad wolf. He was a big sad wolf.

"Why are you sad?" asked the three pink pigs.

"I don't know," said the big sad wolf. "I am sad, but I don't know why."

Read each question. Then read the story again.
Circle the answer.
Write a sentence to answer the last question.

Who did the three pink pigs see?

best   wolf   house

Was the wolf happy?

yes   no   best

Why was the wolf sad?

_____

214

Up or Down?

Some things can go up. Birds can go up. They fly up into the sky.

Some balloons can go up. If you let go, the balloon goes up!

Kites can go up, too. You can fly a kite in the sky.

Some things do not go up. A car does not go up. A dog does not go up. And a truck does not go up.

Read the words. Then read the story again. Write each word where it belongs.

kite   truck   car   bird

They Go Up	They Do Not Go Up
_____	_____
_____	_____

Is It Round?

Some things are round. A ball is round. A ball is very, very round!

A dish can be round, too. So can a cake. A cake can be round.

Some things are not round. Bricks are not round. No, a brick is never round.

Most books are not round. And a house is not round.

Read the words. Then read the story again.
Write each word where it belongs.

brick   dish   cake   book

They Are Round   **They Are Not Round**

_____   _____

_____   _____

216

Cold Cat Finds a Penny

Cold Cat walked along. He looked up and down as he walked. He looked up and saw the sky. Then he looked down and saw a penny.

"A penny," said Cold Cat. "I will pick it up." So he picked up the penny.

Soon Cold Cat saw another penny. He picked up the second penny, too.

Then Cold Cat had two pennies.

Read each question. Then read the story again. Write a sentence to answer each question.

What did Cold Cat see when he looked up?

_____

What did Cold Cat see when he looked down?

_____

How many pennies did Cold Cat pick up?

_____

What do you think Cold Cat will do with the pennies?

_____

The third pink pig looked at the big sad wolf. "Do not be sad," said the third pink pig.

"Come into my house," said the third pink pig. "My house is made of pink bricks. My house will make you happy."

So the big sad wolf went into the brick house.

But it did not make him happy. "This house is too hard," said the big sad wolf. "It is so hard it makes me sad."

Read each question. Then read the story again. Write a sentence to answer each question.

Which pink pig talked to the wolf?

_____

Who said, "Come into my house?"

_____

What kind of house was it?

_____

Why didn't this house make the wolf happy?

_____

218

The Gum House

"Come into my house," said the second pink pig. "My house is made of pink gum. My house will make you happy."

So the wolf went into the gum house.

Just then, rain came down. A lot of rain came down. The rain came into the gum house.

"This house is too wet," said the big sad wolf. "It is so wet it makes me sad. I am still a big sad wolf."

This story is called **The Gum House**.
The Gum House helps tell what the story is about.
Circle two other titles that help tell what the story is about.

Wolf Is Happy   **The Wet House**

The First Pink Pig   **Wolf Is Still Sad**

Write your own title for this story.

_____

Looking for Pennies

Cold Cat walked along. He looked down and saw a third penny. So he picked it up.

Now Cold Cat had three pennies.

Then he found another penny. Now he had four pennies!

Cold cat walked and looked. He looked down, not up.

Cold Cat walked right into a bus. The doors closed. The bus went away.

"Oh, oh," said Cold Cat. "Where am going?"

This story is called **Looking for Pennies**.
Looking for Pennies helps tell what the story is about.
Circle two other titles that help tell what the story is about.

Look Up, Cold Cat   **Cold Cat Is Hot**

Five Pennies   **Where Is Cold Cat Going?**

Write your own title for this story.

_____

Up, Up, and Away!

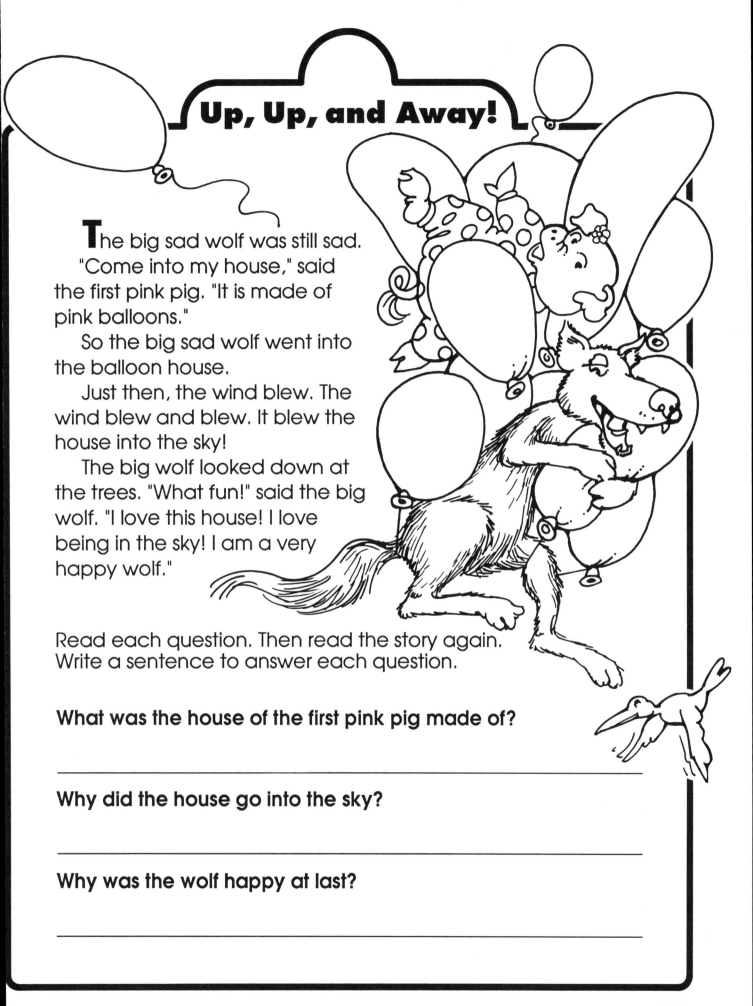

The big sad wolf was still sad. "Come into my house," said the first pink pig. "It is made of pink balloons."

So the big sad wolf went into the balloon house.

Just then, the wind blew. The wind blew and blew. It blew the house into the sky!

The big wolf looked down at the trees. "What fun!" said the big wolf. "I love this house! I love being in the sky! I am a very happy wolf."

Read each question. Then read the story again. Write a sentence to answer each question.

What was the house of the first pink pig made of?

_____

Why did the house go into the sky?

_____

Why was the wolf happy at last?

_____

The Animals

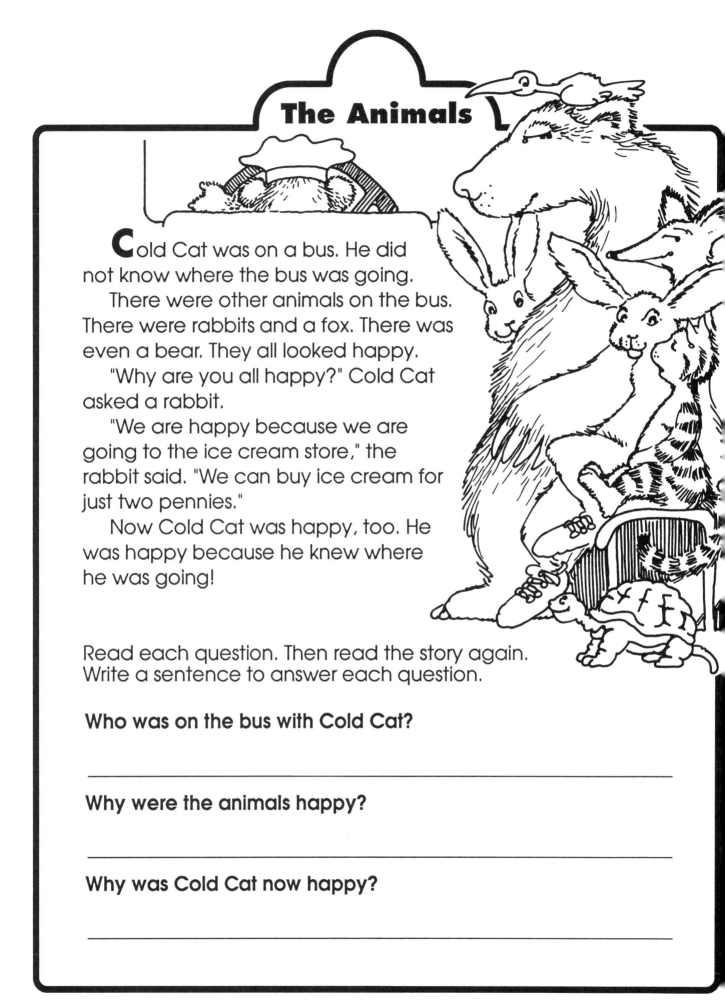

Cold Cat was on a bus. He did not know where the bus was going.

There were other animals on the bus. There were rabbits and a fox. There was even a bear. They all looked happy.

"Why are you all happy?" Cold Cat asked a rabbit.

"We are happy because we are going to the ice cream store," the rabbit said. "We can buy ice cream for just two pennies."

Now Cold Cat was happy, too. He was happy because he knew where he was going!

Read each question. Then read the story again. Write a sentence to answer each question.

Who was on the bus with Cold Cat?

_____

Why were the animals happy?

_____

Why was Cold Cat now happy?

_____

C old Cat looked all around the bus. He saw Hot Dog. But Hot Dog did not look happy. Hot Dog looked sad.

"Why are you sad?" asked Cold Cat. "Don't you like ice cream?"

"I love ice cream," said Hot Dog. "But I lost my pennies. I had four pennies, but I lost them. Now I can't buy ice cream."

"Yes, you can," said Cold Cat. "I found your pennies." Cold Cat gave the four pennies to Hot Dog.

The bus stopped at the ice cream store.

"Come on," said Hot Dog. "I will buy two ice creams. One for you and one for me." And so he did.

Read each question. Then read the story again. Write a sentence to answer each question.

Why was Hot Dog sad?

_____

Why did Cold Cat give the pennies to Hot Dog?

_____

Why was Cold Cat a good friend?

_____

ANSWER KEY

Page 193
dog
no
The dog did
not go away.

Page 194
cars
red
The cake
looks like a
car.

Page 195
2
4
3
1

Page 196
goat
eat
That is what
goats should
eat.

Page 197
dog
dog
Cold Cat is
always cold.

Page 198
father
boy
A fish reads
the book.

Page 199
pink
first
balloon

Page 200
kitten
little
puppy

Page 201
4
2
3
1

Page 202
kid
Cold Cat
A boy or girl
is called a kid.

Page 203
4
2
1
3

Page 204
1
4
3
2

Page 205
Hot Dog
Cold Cat
Hot Dog
Hot Dog cannot
go up a tree.

Page 206
wolf
store
hat
He wanted
to look big.

Page 207
third
bricks
truck

Page 208
home
tigers
zoo

Page 209
Hot Dog got a box.
He put cold water
in the box.
Hot Dog sat in the
cold water.

Page 210
Scott
Ann
Scott
Ann

Page 211
The Three Pink Pigs
Three Pink Houses
Answers will vary.

Page 212
Walking in the Rain
We Are Not Wet

Page 213
Sara needed boots.
Jason wanted yellow
boots.
He did not want
their feet to get wet.

Page 214
wolf
no
The wolf did
not know why.

Page 215
They Go Up
kite
bird
They Do Not Go Up
truck
car

Page 216
They Are Round
dish
cake
They Are Not Round
brick
book

Page 217
Cold Cat saw the sky.
He saw a penny.
He picked up two
pennies.
Answers will vary.

Page 218
The third pink pig
talked to the wolf.
The third pink pig said it.
It was a brick house.
The house was too hard.

Page 219
The Wet House
Wolf Is Still Sad
Answers will vary.

Page 220
Look Up, Cold Cat
Where Is Cold Cat Going?
Answers will vary.

Page 221
It was made of balloons.
The wind blew the
house into the sky.
The wolf liked being
in the sky.

Page 222
There were other
animals on the bus.
They were going
to the ice cream
store.
He knew where he
was going.

Page 223
Hot Dog lost
his pennies.
They were Hot
Dog's pennies.
He gave Hot Dog
the pennies
he found.

Note:
Children's sentences will vary from these in the answer key.
Accept the answer when it is in correct sentence form and answers the question.

Circle the sentence that goes with each picture.

Brave Bear counts the eggs.
Brave Bear carries the eggs.

The goat saw a truck.
The goat saw the turtle.

The elephant eats peanuts.
The elephant sells peanuts.

The rabbit wins the race
Both rabbits win the race.

FINISH LINE

I keep pennies in a jar.
I keep eggs in a basket.

The dragon ate the dish.
The dragon held a candle.

My pocket is in my shoe.
My shoe is in my pocket.

Circle the sentence that goes with each picture.

Dad is high up on the ladder.
Dad is low on the ladder.

Wow! What a big cupcake!
Wow! What a big chicken!

Two lamps moved the lion.
Two lambs moved the lion.

Feathers fell on Brave Bear.
Brave Bear fell on the feathers.

The fence jumped over the horse.
The horse jumped over the fence.

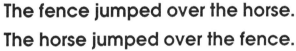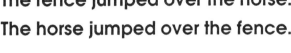

The cat drank milk from a bowl.
Across the street walked the cat.

Brave Bear looks for honey.
Brave Bear hunts for his horn.

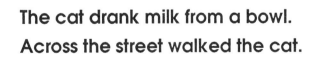

226

Look at each picture and sentence.
Write the correct word on the line.

roof   table   duck   nose   drink   food   watch   puppy

Mom feeds the _____ .

Did you _____ the milkshake?

The telephone is on the _____ .

Brave Bear has a lot of _____ .

Karen found a _____ .

Brave Bear bumped his _____ .

Is this the _____ that Daryl lost?

Brave Bear sat on the _____ .

Look at each picture and sentence.
Write the correct word on the line.

glove   bird   climb   school   prize   blew   kitten   plant

The_____ was in the basket.

Jed took his monkey to _____ .

I won first _____ .

Whose_____ is this?

Alan likes to _____ flowers.

Mr. James_____ the whistle.

Will the clown_____ that pole?

Brave Bear likes the _____ .

228

Read each sentence.
Do what it says.

Draw a **circle** around Brave Bear.

Color the larger shirt **red**.

Color the other shirt **yellow**.

Draw a **box** around the telephone.

Write **L** on the left skate.

Write **R** on the right skate.

Count the whistles.

There are _____ of them.

Read each sentence.
Do what it says.

Draw a **line** from Brave Bear to the picture of the breakfast.

Write an **X** on the picture of the lunch.

Draw a **circle** around the smaller man.

Draw a **box** around the other man.

Write **A** on the picture of the apple pie.

Write **C** on the picture of the cherry pie.

Draw a **pie** and divide it into **four** pieces.

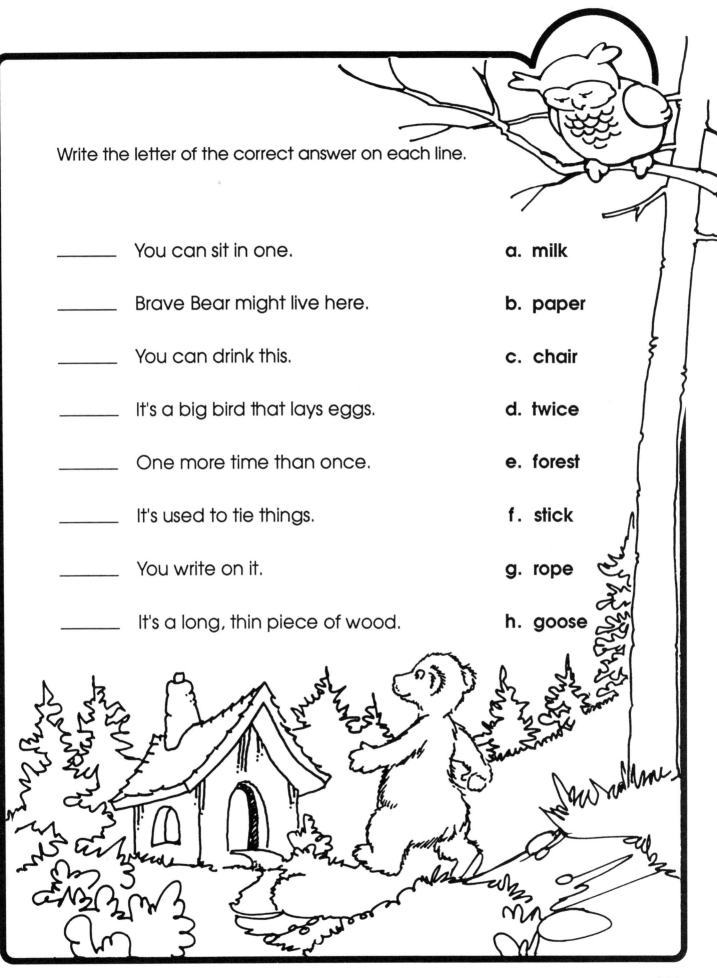

Write the letter of the correct answer on each line.

_____ You can sit in one.

_____ Brave Bear might live here.

_____ You can drink this.

_____ It's a big bird that lays eggs.

_____ One more time than once.

_____ It's used to tie things.

_____ You write on it.

_____ It's a long, thin piece of wood.

a. milk

b. paper

c. chair

d. twice

e. forest

f. stick

g. rope

h. goose

Write the letter of the correct answer on each line.

_____ It's hard and you can walk on it.

_____ Someone who lives next to you is this.

_____ It means not cold, but not very hot.

_____ Fish do this, and so do people.

_____ You can wiggle your toes in this.

_____ You might do this when you sleep.

_____ This comes after the third.

_____ Brave Bear has four of them.

a. warm

b. swim

c. fourth

d. sidewalk

e. dream

f. paws

g. neighbor

h. sand

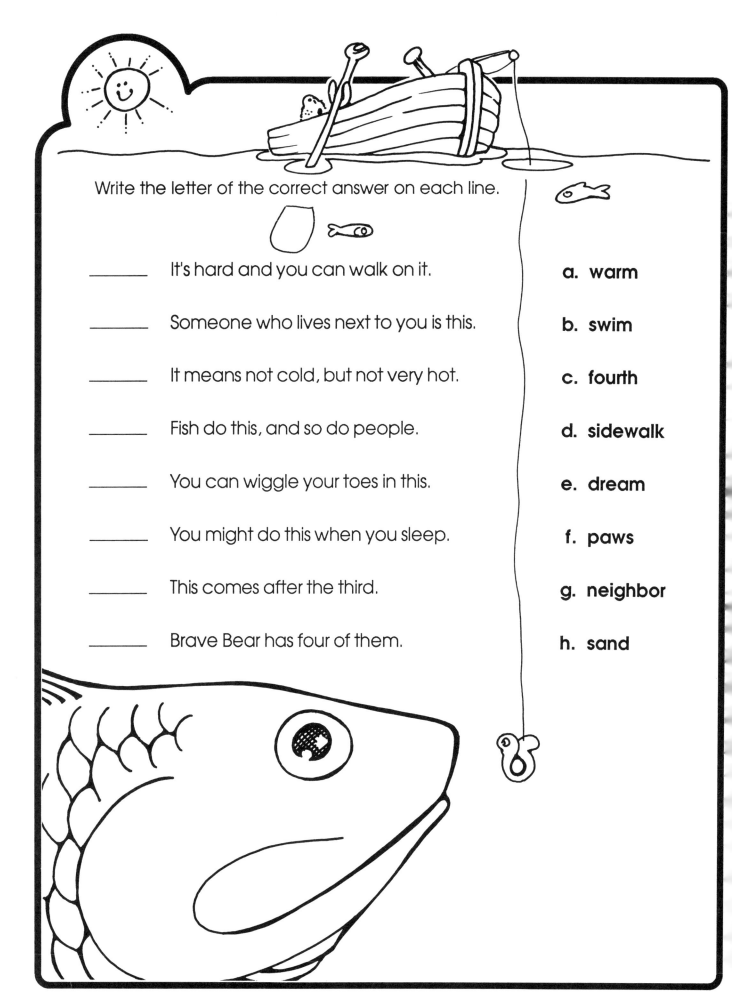

232

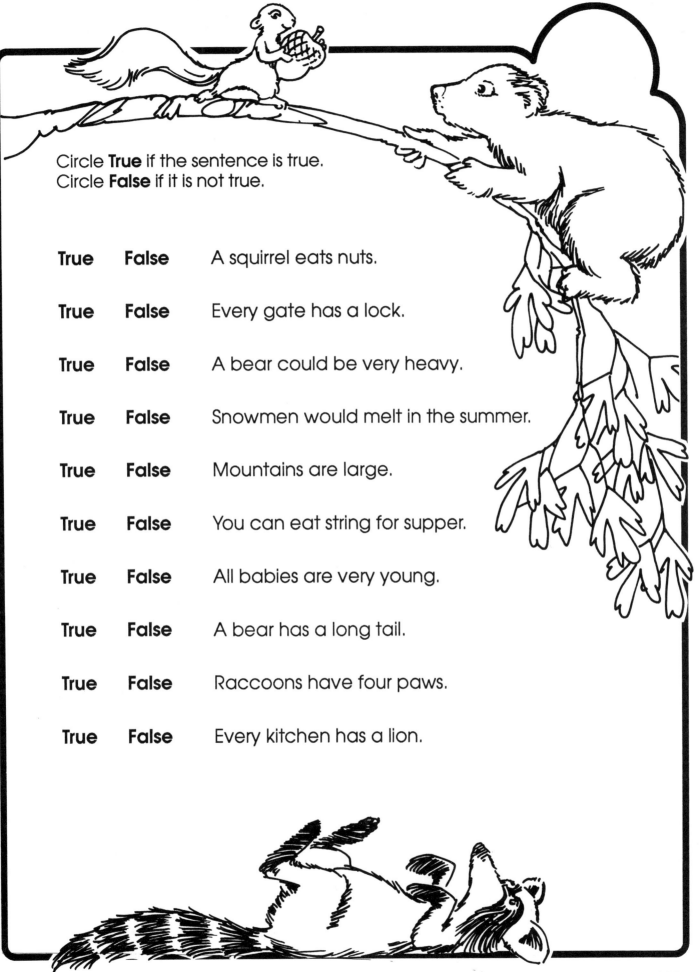

Circle **True** if the sentence is true.
Circle **False** if it is not true.

True   **False**   A squirrel eats nuts.

True   **False**   Every gate has a lock.

True   **False**   A bear could be very heavy.

True   **False**   Snowmen would melt in the summer.

True   **False**   Mountains are large.

True   **False**   You can eat string for supper.

True   **False**   All babies are very young.

True   **False**   A bear has a long tail.

True   **False**   Raccoons have four paws.

True   **False**   Every kitchen has a lion.

Circle **True** if the sentence is true.
Circle **False** if it is not true.

True	False	A face has two eyes, one nose, and two mouths.
True	False	You can cut a pie into pieces.
True	False	A robin is a fish.
True	False	There are two wheels on a bike.
True	False	A bear might drink water from a stream.
True	False	Some people live in apartments.
True	False	You can keep cake in a bottle.
True	False	A sad person is very happy.
True	False	Cows live in a barn or in a field.
True	False	You can bake food in an oven.

Words that rhyme have the same last sound.
Who, zoo, blue, and **you** all rhyme.

Read each sentence at the top of the page.
Write it below the sentence it rhymes with
at the bottom of the page.

Brave Bear shakes the **floor**.

Brave Bear is very **cold**.

He will hide behind the **chair**.

Down the hill he will **go**.

Brave Bear likes to **snore**.

Brave Bear shakes the floor.

Brave Bear likes the **snow**.

_____

Brave Bear looks for **gold**.

_____

Brave Bear doesn't **care**.

_____

Read each sentence at the top
of the page. Write it below the sentence
it rhymes with at the bottom of the page.

Try the tub or sink **instead**.
It's the best that I can **buy**.
What wild, wild sounds we **heard**.
It gives me a big, bad **scare**.
With her is a kangaroo named **Key**.

Two cats brought home a **bird**.

_____

She will sail the deep blue **sea**.

_____

Never hide under the **bed**.

_____

See the look on that **bear**.

_____

I will eat the cherry **pie**.

_____

236

Look at each picture.
Read the question.
Write an **X** next to the sentence that tells the reason why.

Why is Emma happy?

_____ She does not like Yup, her dog.

_____ She must go to school.

_____ She likes her dog Yup, and Yup likes her.

Why is Brave Bear hot?

_____ It is winter.

_____ It is a hot summer day.

_____ He forgot his sunglasses.

Why is Dad tired?

_____ He is carrying heavy things.

_____ He does not like to go camping.

_____ The car is in the garage.

Why isn't Colin in school?

_____ He's going on a trip.

_____ He doesn't feel well.

_____ Today is his birthday.

Why is the dog sad?

_____ The dog does not like trees.

_____ The dog is very sleepy.

_____ The squirrel is dropping shells on it.

Look at each picture.
Read the question.
Write an **X** next to the sentence that tells the reason why.

Why is the parade late?

_____ The float is too big.

_____ A float has a flat tire.

_____ Too many people are in the street.

Why did the turtle win the race?

_____ Turtles run very fast.

_____ The rabbit let it win.

_____ The rabbit fell asleep.

Why are the skates broken?

_____ The elephant was too heavy for them.

_____ The skates were always broken.

_____ The elephant threw them away.

Why is Brave Bear wet?

_____ The rain is falling.

_____ Brave Bear is taking a bath.

_____ Brave Bear is taking a shower.

Why does the cowgirl have a rope?

_____ She wants to jump rope.

_____ She wants to catch the horse.

_____ She wants to fix the fence.

Look at each picture.
Read the question.
Write an **X** next to the sentence that tells the reason why.

Why is Max hurt?

_____ He fell on a bear.

_____ He fell off his bike.

_____ He should have walked home.

Why are the dishes dirty?

_____ The animals buy dirty dishes.

_____ The animals just finished dinner.

_____ The animals sell dirty dishes.

Why is Rosa afraid?

_____ She thinks she lost her dress.

_____ The closet is full of coats and shoes.

_____ She thinks a monster is in the closet.

Why does the woman scold Brave Bear?

_____ He ate the apples.

_____ He ate the pies.

_____ She doesn't like bears.

Why is the elevator empty?

_____ The elephants are afraid of the mouse.

_____ The mouse is afraid of the elephants.

_____ The elephants like peanuts.

Look at each picture.
Put an **X** next to the sentences that go with each picture.

_____ The kangaroo is happy.

_____ A plane is in the air.

_____ The bowl is almost empty.

_____ The glass is full.

_____ The kangaroo is outside.

_____ A monkey watches.

_____ The bowl is very full.

_____ The kangaroo is sad.

_____ Two girls walk in the park.

_____ A woman sits on a bench.

_____ There are flowers in the park.

_____ The boy walks his dog.

_____ The woman sits outside.

_____ The boy pulls a wagon.

_____ A man feeds a squirrel.

_____ It is a very cold day.

Look at each picture.
Put an **X** next to the sentences that go with each picture.

____ Mom talks on the telephone.

____ It is early in the morning.

____ It is night time.

____ A toy dog is walking.

____ The baby eats ice cream.

____ The oven door is open.

____ The baby eats a cookie.

____ Dad and Emma help
     make dinner.

____ Brave Bear carries wood.

____ The rabbit laughs.

____ The fox sees birds.

____ The rabbit is not happy.

____ Brave Bear has a basket.

____ The squirrel holds the eggs.

____ A crow chases Brave Bear.

____ The raccoon holds a broom.

Look at each picture.
Put an **X** next to the sentences that go with each picture.

___ The tower is quite tall.

___ In the tower is a princess.

___ The horse has no rider.

___ The princess has long hair.

___ Grass grows around the tower.

___ The rider is very old.

___ The rider sees the princess.

___ There are no windows
    in the tower.

___ All the cars have stopped.

___ Three cars have stopped.

___ Brave Bear drives a car.

___ The policeman has a whistle.

___ The policeman is a woman.

___ Brave Bear holds a box.

___ A truck carries chickens.

___ People are crying.

242

Read each sentence.
Write the correct word on each line.

quiet	hole
tie	listen
pat	empty
send	city
lazy	early

"Please be _____ . Stop making that noise!"

I think the teacher is going to _____ us home.

"Six o'clock in the morning is very _____ ," growled Brave Bear.

_____ ! Do you hear the phone ringing?

I saw the rabbit run into its _____ .

Hold your finger here while I _____ the string.

Oh, oh! The lion's cage is _____ .

If I don't work hard, will you call me _____ ?

"Never _____ a bear on the head," growled Brave Bear.

A farmer does not work in the _____ .

Read each sentence.
Write the correct word on each line.

wing   people

shape   friendly

point   win

flew   library

finish   splash

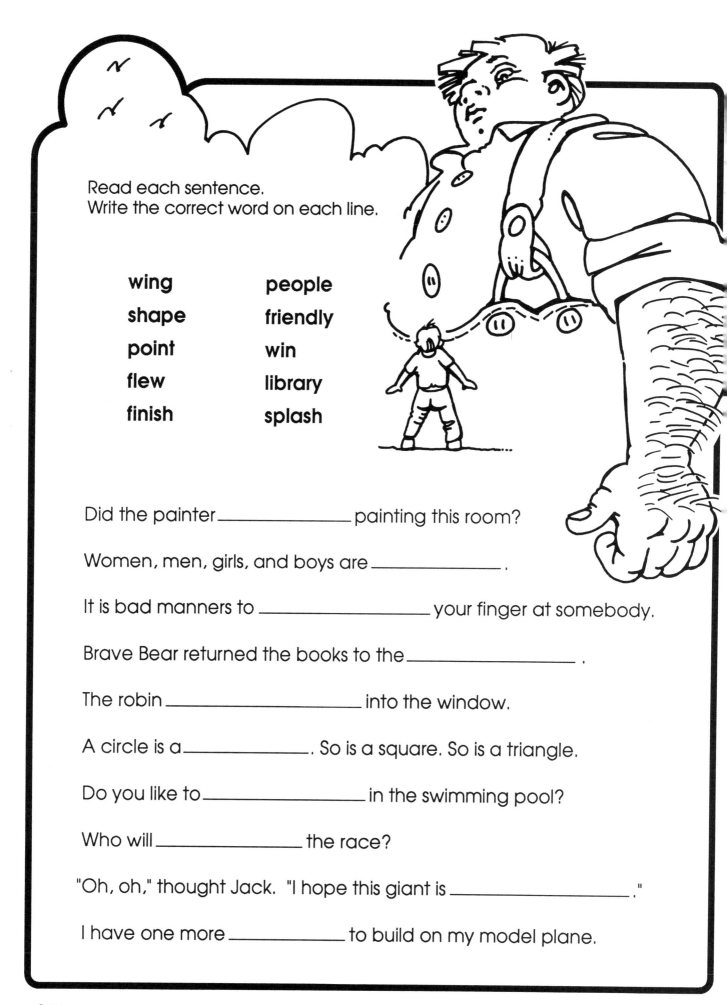

Did the painter_____ painting this room?

Women, men, girls, and boys are _____ .

It is bad manners to _____ your finger at somebody.

Brave Bear returned the books to the_____ .

The robin _____ into the window.

A circle is a_____ . So is a square. So is a triangle.

Do you like to_____ in the swimming pool?

Who will_____ the race?

"Oh, oh," thought Jack. "I hope this giant is _____ ."

I have one more _____ to build on my model plane.

Read each sentence.
Write the correct word on each line.

doctor	branch
drive	tractor
sign	magic
few	bump
clever	remember

Sara's mother will ＿＿＿＿＿＿＿ us to school.

The truck went over the ＿＿＿＿＿＿＿ in the road.

The ＿＿＿＿＿＿＿ gave me a shot.

Mr. Jackson could not ＿＿＿＿＿＿＿ my name.

Brave Bear made a ＿＿＿＿＿＿＿ that said STAY OUT!

Somebody who is very smart is ＿＿＿＿＿＿＿ .

"I want to be a farmer and drive a ＿＿＿＿＿＿＿ ," said Dawn.

This big ＿＿＿＿＿＿＿ fell off that tree.

"We have only a ＿＿＿＿＿＿＿ jars of honey left," said the man.

"It's ＿＿＿＿＿＿＿ ," I said as I pulled a rabbit out of my hat.

Read each question.
Write an **X** next to the sentence that answers the question.

In what way are a boy, a flower, and a bear alike?

_____ They are all green.

_____ All are animals.

_____ All are alive.

In what way are a bridge, a sidewalk, and a floor alike?

_____ You can walk on each of them.

_____ All of them are soft and fluffy.

_____ They are always gray.

In what way are a dollar, a penny, and a dime alike?

_____ They are all made out of silver.

_____ All are square.

_____ They are all money.

In what way are a slide, a seesaw, and a chair alike?

_____ You can sit on each one.

_____ Each is a toy.

_____ You can find them in every house.

In what way are a farmer, a doctor, and a teacher alike?

_____ They are all men.

_____ They all work.

_____ All of them are women.

246

Read each question.
Write an **X** next to the sentence that answers the question.

In what way are a bell, a telephone, and a whistle alike?

_____ They can all make a sound.

_____ All are alive.

_____ You can blow each one.

In what way are a truck, a plane, and a boat alike?

_____ They all have two wings and four wheels.

_____ Every one is made of wood.

_____ Each will take you from one place to another place.

In what way are a notebook, a book, and a newspaper alike?

_____ None of them are paper.

_____ They are all made out of paper.

_____ None of them are white.

In what way are a bear, the dirt, and hair alike?

_____ They are all things to eat or drink.

_____ You have to brush each of them.

_____ Each one could be brown in color.

In what way are an aunt, an uncle, and a grandmother alike?

_____ Each of them is a woman.

_____ They all belong to a family.

_____ All of them go to work every day.

Read each question.
Write an **X** next to the sentence that answers the question.

In what way are a blueberry, corn, and a hamburger alike?

_____ They are all blue.

_____ All are plants.

_____ They are all food.

In what way are a bear, a deer, and a fox alike?

_____ They are always red in color.

_____ They all live in the woods.

_____ They all walk on two legs.

In what way are a basement, a bedroom, and a kitchen alike?

_____ They are cold and wet.

_____ They are parts of a house.

_____ They are all at the top of the stairs.

In what way are a shovel, a rake, and a hammer alike?

_____ Each is a tool.

_____ You can tie a box with each of them.

_____ They are always kept in the attic.

In what way are a monkey, a girl, and a raccoon alike?

_____ Each can hold things with its hands.

_____ They all wear gloves or mittens.

_____ All of them live in the deep, dark forest.

Read each riddle.
Write the correct answer on each line.

station   swish

tower   bounce

gold   answer

lake   beehive

I am the tall, tall part
of a castle or house.

I'm a _____ .

I am where planes land
and many people wait.

I am called a _____ .

I am the way a ball comes up
when it hits the floor.

I'm a _____ .

A tail does this.
A broom does this.
What do they do?

They both go _____ .

I am the home to hundreds
who buzz in and out.

I am a _____ .

A pond is big, but I am bigger.
A rain is wet, but I am wetter.

I'm a _____ .

I am a color and I
am a lost treasure.

I am _____ .

I'm it! It is me!
I am what you're looking for
and what you need.

I am the _____ .

Read each riddle.
Write the correct answer on each line.

myself   **fruit**

garden   **number**

library   **proud**

button   **whisper**

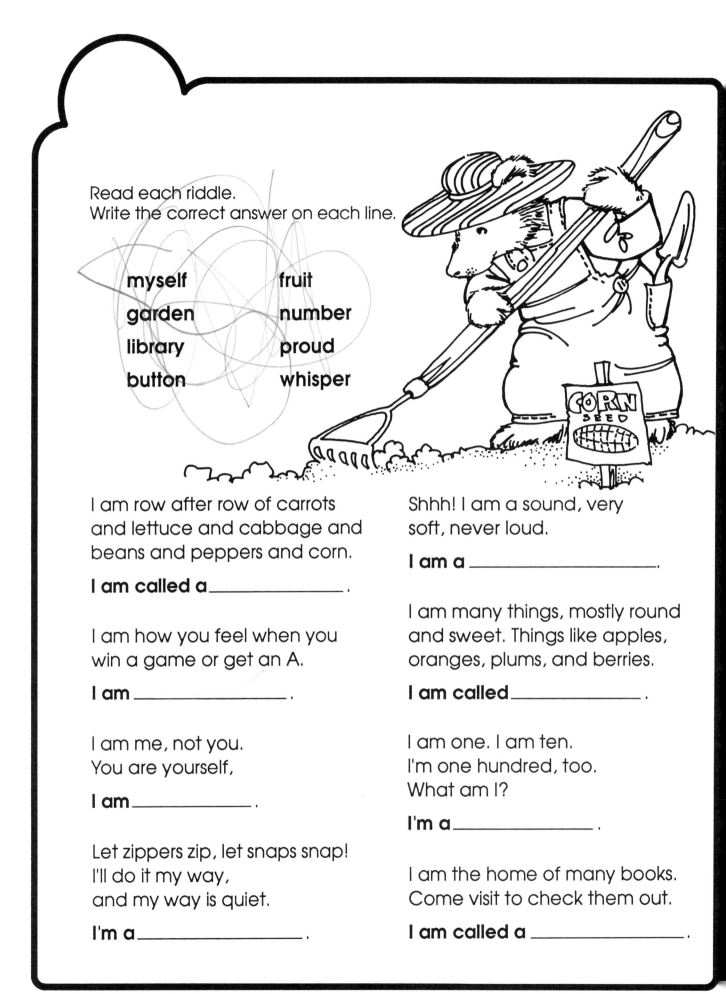

I am row after row of carrots and lettuce and cabbage and beans and peppers and corn.

I am called a_____ .

I am how you feel when you win a game or get an A.

I am _____ .

I am me, not you.
You are yourself,

I am_____ .

Let zippers zip, let snaps snap!
I'll do it my way,
and my way is quiet.

I'm a_____ .

Shhh! I am a sound, very soft, never loud.

I am a _____ .

I am many things, mostly round and sweet. Things like apples, oranges, plums, and berries.

I am called_____ .

I am one. I am ten.
I'm one hundred, too.
What am I?

I'm a_____ .

I am the home of many books.
Come visit to check them out.

I am called a _____ .

250

Read each riddle.
Write the correct answer on each line.

iron   trouble

wrong   sand

above   pair

swan   yard

Sometimes I'm in front,
sometimes in back.
I like to be covered with grass.

I'm a _____ .

Press, press.
I make clothes very smooth.

I am called an _____ .

I am white. I swim.
My neck is very long.

I'm a _____ .

No matter how high you climb,
you will never reach me.

I will always be _____ .

Oh, oh. I am what you
should not get into.

I am _____ .

Left mitten and right mitten.
Salt shaker and pepper shaker.
Two of them make one of me.

I am called a _____ .

You like to walk on me and
wiggle your toes in me, but
you don't like me in your shoes.

I am _____ .

I am never right.
I am never correct.

I am always _____ .

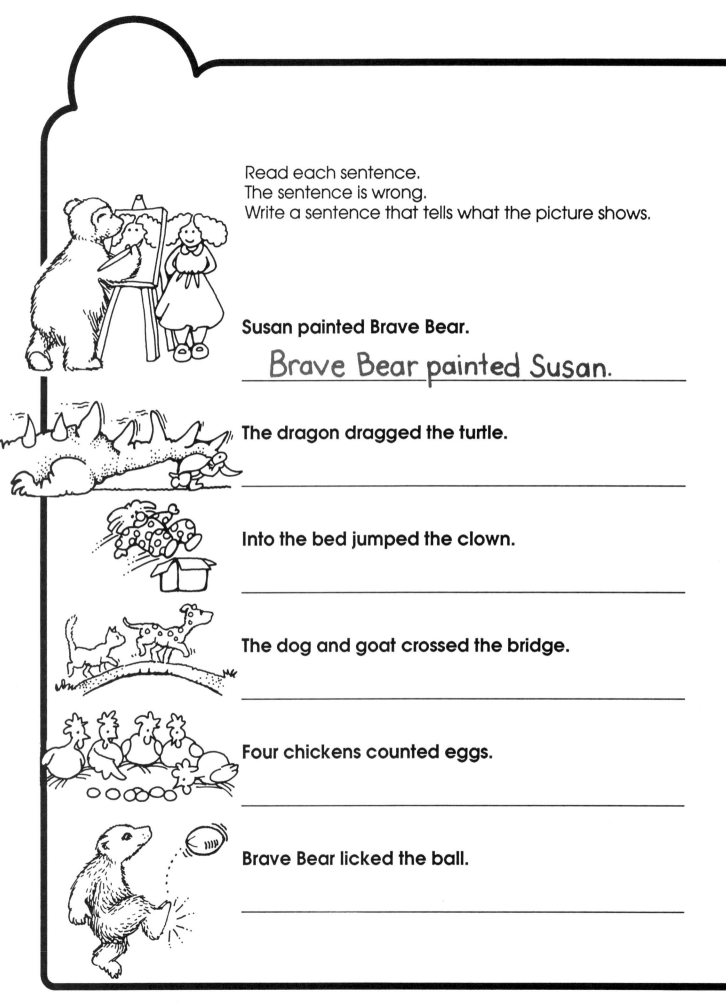

Read each sentence.
The sentence is wrong.
Write a sentence that tells what the picture shows.

Susan painted Brave Bear.

Brave Bear painted Susan.

The dragon dragged the turtle.

_____

Into the bed jumped the clown.

_____

The dog and goat crossed the bridge.

_____

Four chickens counted eggs.

_____

Brave Bear licked the ball.

_____

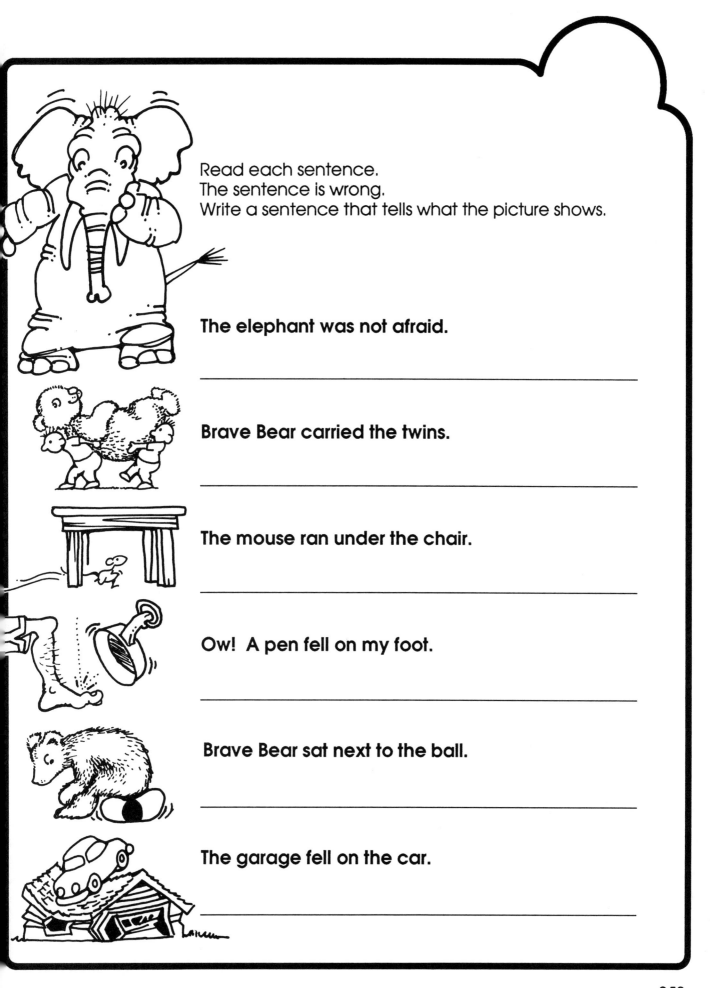

Read each sentence.
The sentence is wrong.
Write a sentence that tells what the picture shows.

The elephant was not afraid.

_____

Brave Bear carried the twins.

_____

The mouse ran under the chair.

_____

Ow! A pen fell on my foot.

_____

Brave Bear sat next to the ball.

_____

The garage fell on the car.

_____

Read each sentence.
The sentence is wrong.
Write a sentence that tells what the picture shows.

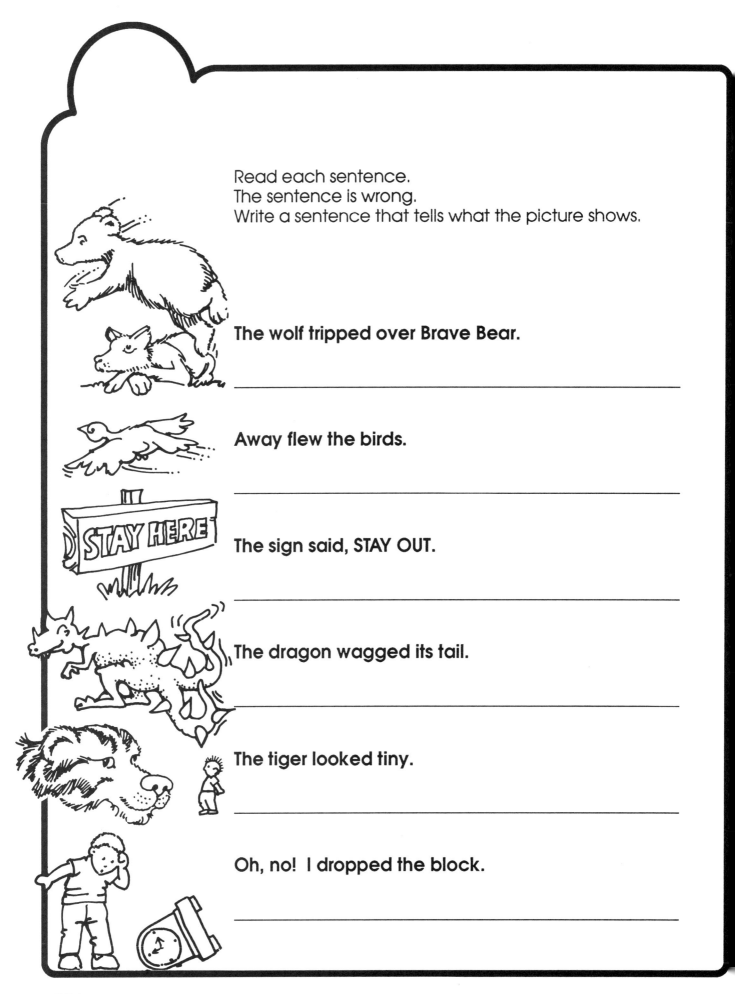

The wolf tripped over Brave Bear.

_____

Away flew the birds.

_____

The sign said, STAY OUT.

_____

The dragon wagged its tail.

_____

The tiger looked tiny.

_____

Oh, no! I dropped the block.

_____

ANSWER KEY

Page 225
Brave Bear counts the eggs.
The goat saw the turtle.
The elephant sells peanuts.
Both rabbits win the race.
I keep pennies in a jar.
The dragon held a candle.
My shoe is in my pocket.

Page 226
Dad is low on the ladder.
Wow! What a big cupcake!
Two lambs moved the lion.
Feathers fell on Brave Bear.
The horse jumped over the fence.
The cat drank milk from a bowl.
Brave Bear hunts for his horn.

Page 227
duck
drink
table
food
puppy
nose
watch
roof

Page 228
kitten
school
prize
glove
plant
blew
climb
bird

Page 229
6 (whistles)

Page 231
c
e
a
h
d
g
b
f

Page 232
d
g
a
b
h
e
c
f

Page 233
True
False
True
True
True
False
True
False
True
False

Page 234
False
True
False
True
True
False
False
True
True

Page 235
Brave Bear shakes the floor.
Down the hill he will go.
Brave Bear is very cold.
He will hide behind the chair.

Page 236
What wild, wild sounds we heard.
With her is a kangaroo named Key.
Try the tub or sink instead.
It gives me a big, bad scare.
It's the best that I can buy.

Page 237
She likes her dog Yup,
and Yup likes her.
It is a hot summer day.
He is carrying heavy things.
He doesn't feel well.
The squirrel is dropping
shells on it.

Page 238
A float has a flat tire.
The rabbit fell asleep.
The elephant was too
heavy for them.
Brave Bear is taking a shower.
She wants to catch the horse.

Page 239
He fell off his bike.
The animals just finished dinner.
She thinks a monster is in the closet.
He ate the apples.
The elephants are afraid
of the mouse.

Page 240
The kangaroo is happy.
The glass is full.
A monkey watches.
The bowl is very full.

A woman sits on a bench.
There are flowers in the park.
The boy walks his dog.
The woman sits outside.
A man feeds a squirrel.

Page 241
It is night time.
A toy dog is walking.
The oven door is open.
The baby eats a cookie.
Dad and Emma help make dinner.

Brave Bear carries wood.
The rabbit laughs.
The fox sees birds.
Brave Bear has a basket.
The raccoon holds a broom.

Page 242
The tower is quite tall.
In the tower is a princess.
The princess has long hair.
Grass grows around the tower.
The rider sees the princess.

Three cars have stopped.
The policeman has a whistle.
Brave Bear holds a box.
A truck carries chickens.

Page 243
quiet
send
early
Listen
hole
tie
empty
lazy
pat
city

Page 244
finish
people
point
library
flew
shape
splash
win
friendly
wing

Page 245
drive
bump
doctor
remember
sign
clever
tractor
branch
few
magic

Page 246
All are alive.
You can walk on
each of them.
They are all money.
You can sit on each one.
They all work.

Page 247
They can all make a sound.
Each will take you from one place
to another place.
They are all made out of paper.
Each one could be brown in color.
They all belong to a family.

Page 248
They are all food.
They all live in the woods.
They are parts of a house.
Each is a tool.
Each can hold things
with its hands.

Page 249
tower; beehive
airport; lake
bounce; gold
swish; answer

Page 250
garden; whisper
proud; fruit
myself; number
button; library

Page 251
yard; trouble
iron; pair
swan; sand
above; wrong

Page 252
Brave Bear painted Susan.
The turtle dragged the dragon.
Into the box jumped the clown.
The dog and cat crossed
the bridge.
Five chickens counted eggs.
Brave Bear kicked the ball.

Page 253
The elephant was afraid.
The twins carried Brave Bear.
The mouse ran under the table.
Ow! A pan fell on my foot.
Brave Bear sat on the ball.
The car fell on the garage.

Page 254
Brave Bear tripped over the wolf.
OR: The wolf tripped Brave Bear.
Away flew the bird.
The sign said, STAY HERE.
The dragon wagged its tails.
The tiger looked big. (huge/large)
Oh, no! I dropped the clock.

What a House

Words that rhyme have the same last sound.
Do, **shoe**, and **blue** all rhyme.
Write in the missing words to finish the story.
Write in the word that rhymes with the **bold** word.

bed   **house**   **honey**   **door**   **pet**

One day a **mouse**

Moved into Brave Bear's __house__.

Brave Bear slept on the **floor.**

Right next to the _____.

"Move right in," Brave Bear **said.**

"Find a place to put your _____."

"You'll find the bath is always **wet,**

Because I keep a whale as a _____."

"Things around here are always **funny.**

Take what you want, but don't take my _____."

Good Morning, Rabbit

Rabbit hears the clock. The clock is ringing. The sound wakes Rabbit up. He opens one eye. He looks at the clock. "Oh," says Rabbit. "Oh, no."

Then Rabbit rolls over. He still hears the clock ringing. So Rabbit sits up. He fold his big ears over. Now he cannot hear the clock. He goes back to sleep.

Somebody is shaking Rabbit – shaking him hard. He opens one eye. Oh, oh. It is Mother Rabbit. "Are you still sleeping?" She asks. "It is time to brush your teeth. It is time to eat breakfast. You are going to be late for school. Then I will not be happy."

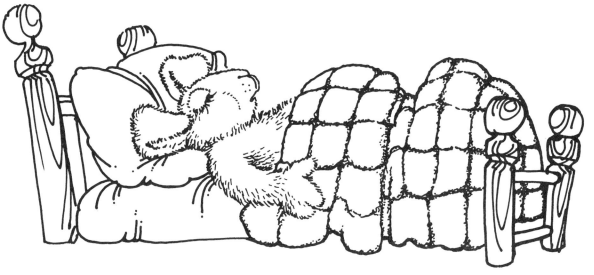

Read each question below.
Write a sentence to answer each question.

Who is sleeping?

_____

What wakes Rabbit up?

_____

What does Rabbit fold over?

_____

Who shakes Rabbit?

_____

One, Two, Tree!

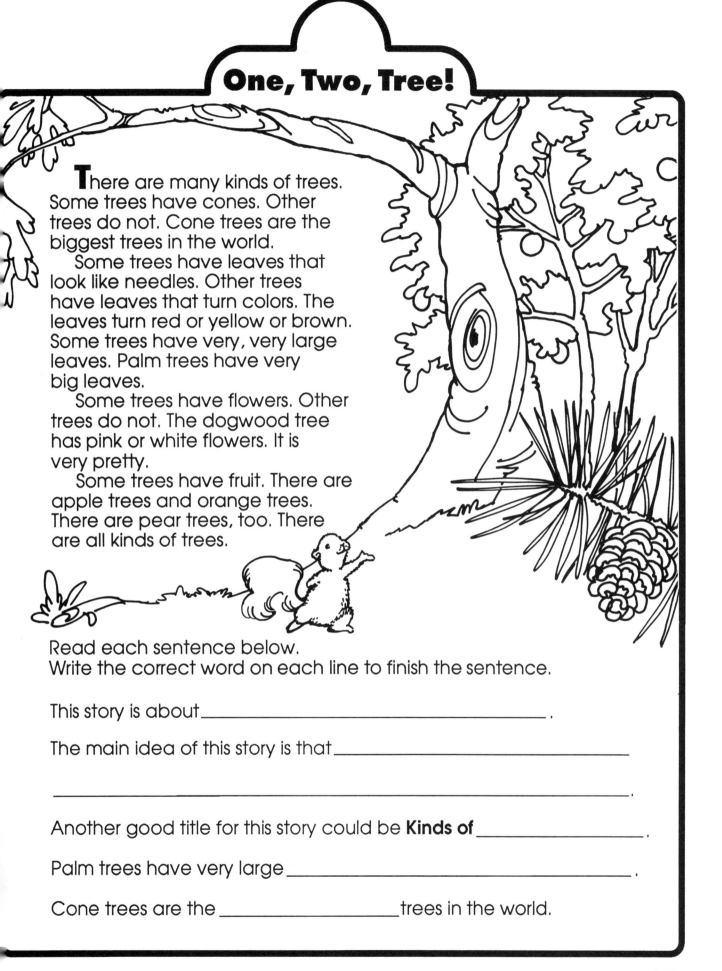

There are many kinds of trees. Some trees have cones. Other trees do not. Cone trees are the biggest trees in the world.

Some trees have leaves that look like needles. Other trees have leaves that turn colors. The leaves turn red or yellow or brown. Some trees have very, very large leaves. Palm trees have very big leaves.

Some trees have flowers. Other trees do not. The dogwood tree has pink or white flowers. It is very pretty.

Some trees have fruit. There are apple trees and orange trees. There are pear trees, too. There are all kinds of trees.

Read each sentence below.
Write the correct word on each line to finish the sentence.

This story is about_____ .

The main idea of this story is that_____

_____ .

Another good title for this story could be **Kinds of** _____ .

Palm trees have very large _____ .

Cone trees are the _____ trees in the world.

Brave Bear Digs

Brave Bear looked around his house. "I have a lot of honey," he said. "I need more space for my honey!" He thought a while. "I will dig a basement," he said. "Then I will have more space."

Brave Bear went into his bedroom. "This is where I will begin," he said. "I will dig straight down. Then I will have a basement."

"That is not correct," said Owl, who was there. "That is not correct."

But Brave Bear did not listen to Owl. No, Brave Bear dug. He dug in the bedroom. Soon he had a basement where his bedroom had been. Then he moved into another room. Brave Bear dug straight down through his whole house. "There," he said at last. "I have finished! I will keep my honey in the basement."

But when Brave Bear looked, all he saw was basement. "Where is my house?" shouted Brave Bear.

"It is in your basement," said Owl. "To dig a basement, you must dig under your house. You must not dig straight down through your house."

Read each question and circle the correct answer.

Where does Brave Bear begin to dig?
basement   bedroom   hall

Does he dig straight down through the house?
yes   no   never

Who says, "That is not correct"?
Brave Bear   Owl   Honey

What does Brave Bear need more of?
honey   space   basement

What does Brave Bear have a lot of?
space   Owl   honey

The Dog and the Duck

Words that rhyme have the same last sound.
Do, **shoe**, and **blue** all rhyme.
Write in the missing words to finish the story.
Write in the word that rhymes with the **bold** word.

truck   **log**   **luck**   **bone**   **jog**

One day a duck and a **dog**

Sat in the woods on a _____.

The dog said, "Here we are **alone**.

I don't even have a _____."

"We are lost," said the **duck**.

"What bad _____."

"I must go," said the **dog**.

"I can get home if I _____."

"Not me," said the **duck**.

"I always go home in a _____."

Corn

Corn is a plant. It grows very tall. Most corn is yellow. People cook corn and eat it.

Corn grows on a cob. Many people eat corn on the cob. Some people take the corn off the cob. Then they eat the little pieces of corn.

There are other ways to eat corn. Some corn can be made into popcorn. First, the corn must be dry. Then it is cooked. When it gets very hot, it pops. The corn pops into popcorn.

Some people grind dry corn. Then the corn looks like dry yellow powder. This powder is called meal. Corn that looks like this is cornmeal. Some people cook cornmeal in water and eat it. Some people make it into pancakes and eat it. There are many, many ways to eat corn.

Read each question. Then read the story a second time. Circle the correct answer.

What is corn?

      animal   plant   popcorn

When you grind dry corn, what is it called?

      cornmeal   oatmeal   breakfast

What color is most corn?

      white   red   yellow

Many people eat corn on the _____.

      cob   plant   cap

Some kinds of corn will _____ when cooked.

      stop   pop   grow

262

Brave Bear Bakes

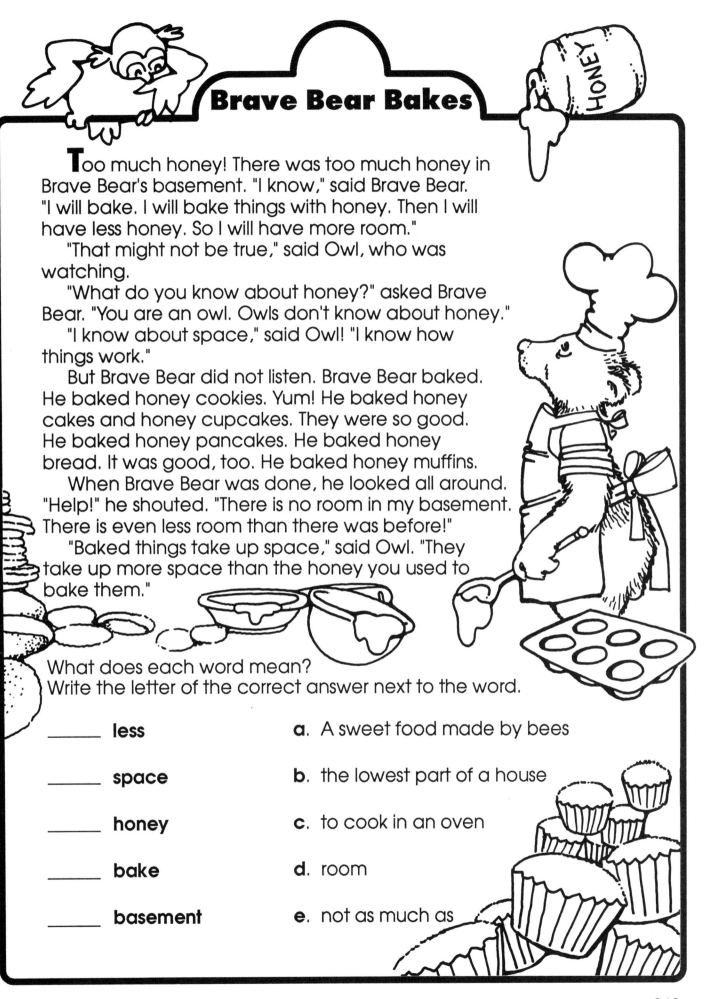

Too much honey! There was too much honey in Brave Bear's basement. "I know," said Brave Bear. "I will bake. I will bake things with honey. Then I will have less honey. So I will have more room."

"That might not be true," said Owl, who was watching.

"What do you know about honey?" asked Brave Bear. "You are an owl. Owls don't know about honey."

"I know about space," said Owl! "I know how things work."

But Brave Bear did not listen. Brave Bear baked. He baked honey cookies. Yum! He baked honey cakes and honey cupcakes. They were so good. He baked honey pancakes. He baked honey bread. It was good, too. He baked honey muffins.

When Brave Bear was done, he looked all around. "Help!" he shouted. "There is no room in my basement. There is even less room than there was before!"

"Baked things take up space," said Owl. "They take up more space than the honey you used to bake them."

What does each word mean?
Write the letter of the correct answer next to the word.

_____ **less**   **a.** A sweet food made by bees

_____ **space**   **b.** the lowest part of a house

_____ **honey**   **c.** to cook in an oven

_____ **bake**   **d.** room

_____ **basement**   **e.** not as much as

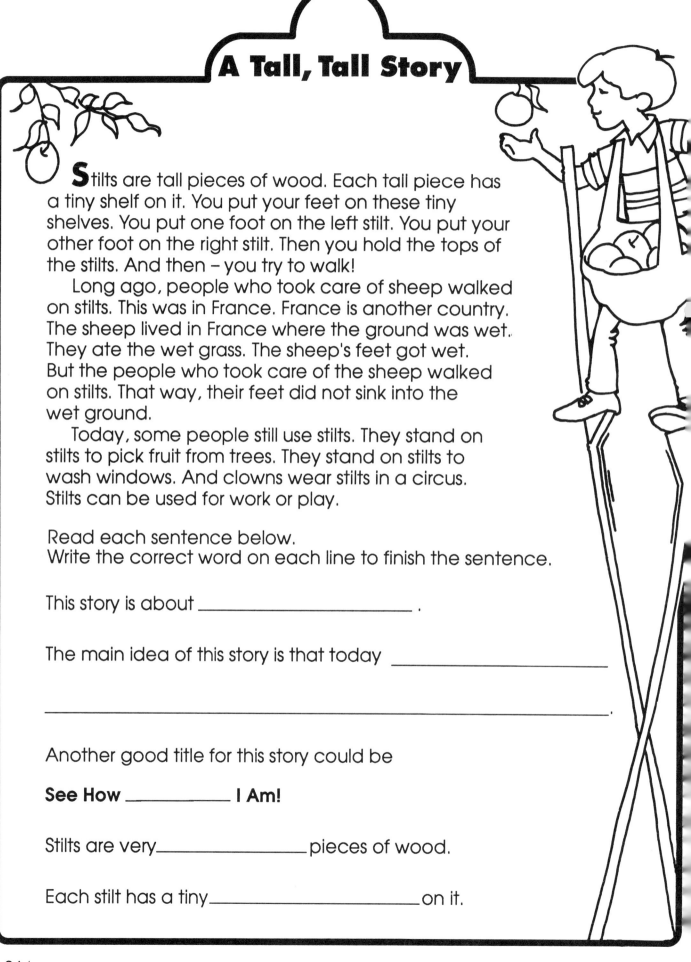

A Tall, Tall Story

Stilts are tall pieces of wood. Each tall piece has a tiny shelf on it. You put your feet on these tiny shelves. You put one foot on the left stilt. You put your other foot on the right stilt. Then you hold the tops of the stilts. And then – you try to walk!

Long ago, people who took care of sheep walked on stilts. This was in France. France is another country. The sheep lived in France where the ground was wet. They ate the wet grass. The sheep's feet got wet. But the people who took care of the sheep walked on stilts. That way, their feet did not sink into the wet ground.

Today, some people still use stilts. They stand on stilts to pick fruit from trees. They stand on stilts to wash windows. And clowns wear stilts in a circus. Stilts can be used for work or play.

Read each sentence below.
Write the correct word on each line to finish the sentence.

This story is about _____ .

The main idea of this story is that today _____

_____.

Another good title for this story could be

See How _____ I Am!

Stilts are very_____pieces of wood.

Each stilt has a tiny_____on it.

The Fox and the Ox

Words that rhyme have the same last sound.
Do, **shoe**, and **blue** all rhyme.

Write in the missing words to finish the story.
Write in the word that rhymes with the **bold** word.

you   box   blocks   door   better

"I spell my name **f o x**," said **Fox**.

"I spell my name with just three_____ ."

"I do not need a fourth **letter**.

Having only three is _____ ."

"I am smart. I can spell cat, dog, and **fox**.

They rhyme with bat, log, and _____ ."

The ox said, "If three is better than **four**,

Then I will throw one letter out the _____ ."

"I can spell my name with just **two**,

So that makes me smarter than _____ ."

Turtle opened one eye. Dark. It was very dark. Turtle opened her other eye. It was still dark. Why was it dark? Turtle didn't remember where she was.

Turtle could hardly move. Her head was resting on one of her front feet. She moved the front foot. Her other front foot was all folded up. Her two back feet were folded up.

It was dark and there was hardly any room. Oh, yes! Now Turtle remembered. She was all inside her shell!

Turtle slowly pushed her head out. Wow! It was bright. There was sunshine all over.

She slowly pushed each foot out. One, two, three, four. Now Turtle was ready to go.

Slowly, Turtle walked down to the river. She ate a bug on the way. She ate some grass, too.

Oh, oh! What was that sound? It was a dog or a fox!

Turtle pulled her head back into her shell. She pulled her feet in, too.

Outside, she saw a red fox. It tried to bite her shell. Ha! Her shell was very hard. No fox could bite it.

Turtle stayed inside her shell. The fox went away.

Then Turtle put her head and feet out. She went down to the river.

266

Circle **True** if a sentence is true.
Circle **False** if it is not true.

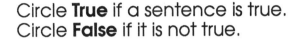

True	**False**	A dog tries to bite Turtle.
True	**False**	Turtle is going to the river.
True	**False**	Turtle eats a bug.
True	**False**	This story is about a fox and a dog.
True	**False**	Another good title for this story is **Safe Inside a Shell**.
True	**False**	**Folded** means **wet**.
True	**False**	When you **bite** something, you put your teeth into it.
True	**False**	First Turtle sees the fox, then she hears it.
True	**False**	Turtles can move very fast.
True	**False**	A turtle's shell keeps it safe from other animals.

The Octopus

The octopus lives in the sea. Octopuses live in seas all over the world. Some octopuses are very small. Some are large. They can be three feet long.

An octopus has a very large head. It has two eyes. Inside the head is a large brain. This means that an octopus can learn. The head is the center of the octopus's body. Around the head are eight arms.

An octopus lives alone, in the crack of a rock. It can squeeze itself into a very small space. This helps it hide from larger animals. Another thing that helps it hide is ink. If something is chasing an octopus, the octopus squirts black ink. The animal chasing it can't see anything but ink.

An octopus hunts for food in the ocean. It eats shellfish. The octopus is a fast hunter. It is a strong hunter, too. When an octopus sees a shellfish, it jumps on top of the shell! Then it pulls open the shell with its strong arms.

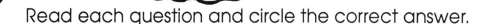

Read each question and circle the correct answer.

Where do octopuses live?

sand   sea   ink

What is at the center of an octopus's body?

eyes   arms   head

What do octopuses eat?

ink   arms   shellfish

How do they get away from other animals?

They squirt ink.   They jump.   They hunt.

How can an octopus hide?

It can jump.   It can squeeze into cracks.   It can eat.

268

Seven Sheep

One day seven sheep wanted to play.
"Let's play a game," said the first sheep. "Let's play follow the leader. I will be the leader first. I will skip across this bridge." The first sheep skipped and the other six sheep followed.

Then it was the second sheep's turn. It ran up a hill and the other six sheep followed. Then the third sheep rolled down the hill and the other sheep followed.

When it was the fourth sheep's turn, it jumped into a large pile of hay. The other six sheep followed.

The fifth sheep was covered with hay. So it ran through a waterfall to get clean. The other sheep followed.

"I will leap over the fence," said the sixth sheep. And so it did. It leaped over the fence and the other sheep followed.

Finally it was the seventh sheep's turn. The seventh sheep found a soft spot in the grass. It lay down on the soft spot. It went to sleep. So did the other sheep.

What does each word mean?
Write the letter of the correct answer next to the word.

_____ **leader**		**a.** water that falls from a high place
_____ **waterfall**		**b.** someone who goes first
_____ **leap**		**c.** to come after or go after
_____ **skip**		**d.** jump
_____ **follow**		**e.** to step and hop

Row, Row, Row Your Boat

Rabbit went down to the river. There were two blue boats in the water. They looked the same. Rabbit got into one of the boats. He began to row down the river. What fun!

Rabbit sang as he rowed. "Row, row, row your boat," he sang. Those were the only words Rabbit knew. That is why he sang them over and over.

Rabbit looked up the river. He saw Brave Bear. Brave Bear was rowing down the river. Brave Bear was rowing the other blue boat very fast.

"Row, row, row your boat," sang Rabbit. He watched Brave Bear row. Soon Brave Bear was even with Rabbit.

"Stop!" shouted Brave Bear.

"Row, row, row your boat," sang Rabbit.

Brave Bear put a paw on Rabbit's boat. "Yes," said Brave Bear. "You can row, row, row *your* boat. But that is *my* boat you are rowing."

Rabbit looked at his boat. It looked like his own blue boat. But then, Brave Bear's boat looked the same. "How can you tell?" asked Rabbit.

"What is in the front of the boat?" asked Brave Bear.

Rabbit looked at the front of the boat. Honey. There were many jars of honey in the boat.

"See," said Brave Bear. "Now, what is in the front of this blue boat?"

Rabbit looked. There were carrots in the front of Brave Bear's blue boat. So Rabbit gave Brave Bear back his boat.

"Row, row, row *my* boat," sang Rabbit as he rowed down the river.

270

Write an **X** by the answer that tells why something happened.

Why does Brave Bear shout, "Stop?"

_____ Brave Bear does not like blue boats.

_____ Rabbit has taken Brave Bear's blue boat.

_____ Brave Bear rows very fast.

How can Brave Bear tell which boat is his?

_____ The boats are different colors.

_____ His boat is red.

_____ His boat has honey in the front.

Why did Rabbit take the wrong boat?

_____ The boats looked alike.

_____ Rabbit likes the color blue.

_____ Rabbit did not like Brave Bear.

Why does Rabbit sing only "Row, row, row your boat?"

_____ He does not know the rest of the words.

_____ He does not like the rest of the words.

_____ Singing makes him row faster.

At the end, why does Rabbit row the boat that has carrots in it?

_____ Rabbit does not like honey.

_____ The boat with carrots is his boat.

_____ The boat with carrots is orange.

At the end, why does Rabbit sing, "Row, row, row my boat?"

_____ He knows all the words.

_____ Brave Bear likes those words the best.

_____ Rabbit is in his own boat.

Down, Down, Down

Otter's mother taught him many things. She taught him all about the water. She taught him how to swim. His mother taught him how to dive for fish. Otter really liked diving for fish. He liked eating them even more.

That's not all. Otter's mother taught him all about the land, too. He learned how to catch snakes and frogs. Otters are very long animals. They have short legs and are close to the ground. So it was easy for Otter to move along the ground quickly. It was easy for him to catch snakes and frogs.

Now his mother wanted to teach him something new. Otter wasn't sure he would like it. Something strange had happened to the land. It was covered with white powder. The powder was cold. Otter's mother went to the top of a hill. Zoom! She slid down the hill on her belly! Now she waited at the bottom of the hill. Otter knew it was his turn to do the same thing. Would he like it?

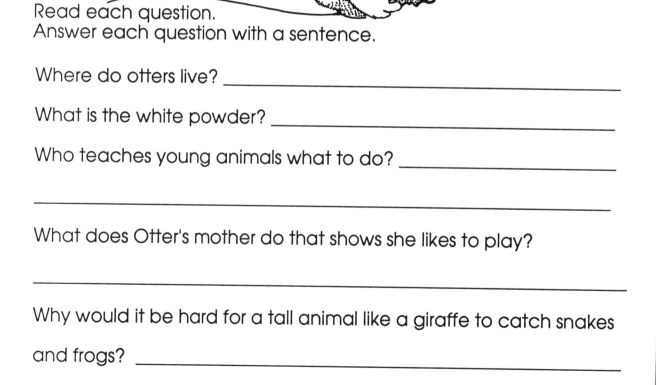

Read each question.
Answer each question with a sentence.

Where do otters live? _____

What is the white powder? _____

Who teaches young animals what to do? _____

_____

What does Otter's mother do that shows she likes to play?

_____

Why would it be hard for a tall animal like a giraffe to catch snakes

and frogs? _____

272

Do You Have Change for a Cow?

Long ago, people did not use money. They did not have pennies or nickels. They did not have dimes or quarters.

There was no money anywhere. So people did not pay for what they wanted. Suppose that Jane wanted shoes. There was no money, so how could Jane get the shoes? Here is how. Jane would trade for the shoes. To trade is to give somebody one thing if that person gives you another thing.

People traded things. Jane traded what she had for what she wanted. Suppose Jane had honey. But she wanted shoes. The person who had shoes wanted honey. So Jane and the other person would trade honey for shoes.

After a long time, animals were used like money. A cow was worth just so much. After animals came corn. It was used like money. Then came sea shells. At long last, somebody made money out of metal. They made coins like we have today. It's a lot easier to carry coins than to carry a cow.

Read each sentence below.
Write the correct word on each line to finish the sentence.

This story is about _____ .

The main idea of this story is that long ago people did not

_____ .

Another good title for this story could be

Different Kinds of _____ .

Before people had coins, they would _____

for what they wanted.

Why do people use money today? _____

_____

Shooting Stars

Have you ever heard of shooting stars? Sometimes you can see them at night. They move across the sky very fast. A trail of light glows behind them. Shooting stars are beautiful to see. But they are not really stars.

A shooting star is a piece of rock from outer space. For many years, the rock spins around in space. When it is out there, in space, it doesn't glow. It has no trail of light.

But as the rock spins, it comes closer and closer to Earth. One day, it comes so close that it falls through our air.

The rock falls very, very fast. As it falls, it makes heat. This heat makes the rock burn. The trail of light is really fire. If the rock falls at night, you can see it burning in the sky. It looks like a bright star that is falling. That is why it is called a shooting star.

Some shooting stars burn themselves up. There is nothing left. But some hit the ground before they burn up. Then the rock makes a hole in the ground.

Read each question.
Write an **X** next to the sentence that answers it.

What happens before the rock falls through our air?

_____ It spins around in space.

_____ It makes a hole in the ground.

What happens before the rock burns away?

_____ It makes a hole in the ground.

_____ It comes very close to Earth and begins to fall.

What happens after the rock comes very close to Earth?

_____ It falls through the air.

_____ It spins around in space.

What happens as the rock falls?

_____ It comes very close to Earth.

_____ It burns.

Do You Believe It?

"Look at that corn!" said Richard. "It's really growing fast."

"It sure is," said his cousin Tanya. Tanya lived on a farm. Richard was from the city. "Corn grows fast in hot weather," she said.

"It sure has been hot," Richard said. He added more ice to his lemonade. "Is it always this hot in the country?"

"Oh, this is nothing," said Tanya. "Last summer it was much hotter. Last summer, it was so hot that the corn in the fields started to pop. It popped right in the field! Big white puffy pieces of corn fell everywhere."

"Really?" asked Richard.

"Sure," answered Tanya. "The pigs and cows saw the big puffy pieces of corn. They thought it was snow. They thought they were in a blizzard! They got so cold that they froze to death."

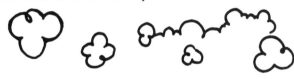

Circle **True** if a sentence is most likely true.
Circle **False** if it is most likely false.
Write a sentence to answer the last question.

True   **False**   Tanya is telling Richard a true story.

True   **False**   When it gets cold, it snows popcorn.

True   **False**   Tanya is having fun with Richard.

True   **False**   This story is mainly about cows and pigs.

Why could the title of this story be "Tanya's Joke"?_____

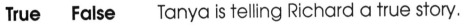

_____

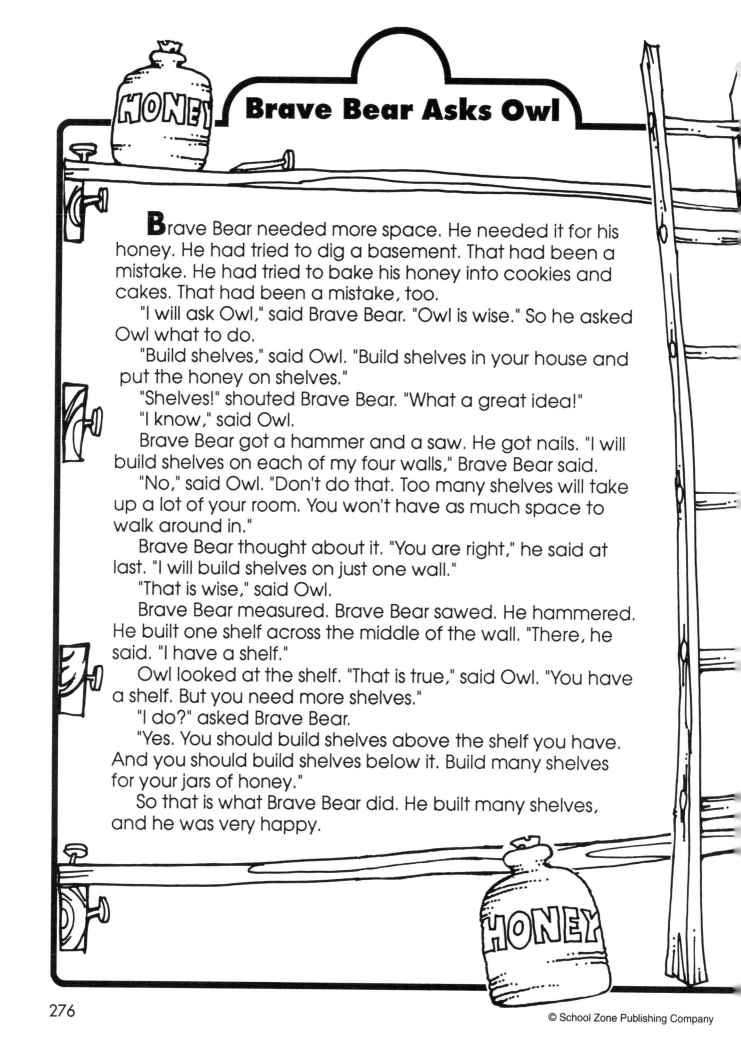

Brave Bear Asks Owl

Brave Bear needed more space. He needed it for his honey. He had tried to dig a basement. That had been a mistake. He had tried to bake his honey into cookies and cakes. That had been a mistake, too.

"I will ask Owl," said Brave Bear. "Owl is wise." So he asked Owl what to do.

"Build shelves," said Owl. "Build shelves in your house and put the honey on shelves."

"Shelves!" shouted Brave Bear. "What a great idea!"

"I know," said Owl.

Brave Bear got a hammer and a saw. He got nails. "I will build shelves on each of my four walls," Brave Bear said.

"No," said Owl. "Don't do that. Too many shelves will take up a lot of your room. You won't have as much space to walk around in."

Brave Bear thought about it. "You are right," he said at last. "I will build shelves on just one wall."

"That is wise," said Owl.

Brave Bear measured. Brave Bear sawed. He hammered. He built one shelf across the middle of the wall. "There, he said. "I have a shelf."

Owl looked at the shelf. "That is true," said Owl. "You have a shelf. But you need more shelves."

"I do?" asked Brave Bear.

"Yes. You should build shelves above the shelf you have. And you should build shelves below it. Build many shelves for your jars of honey."

So that is what Brave Bear did. He built many shelves, and he was very happy.

276

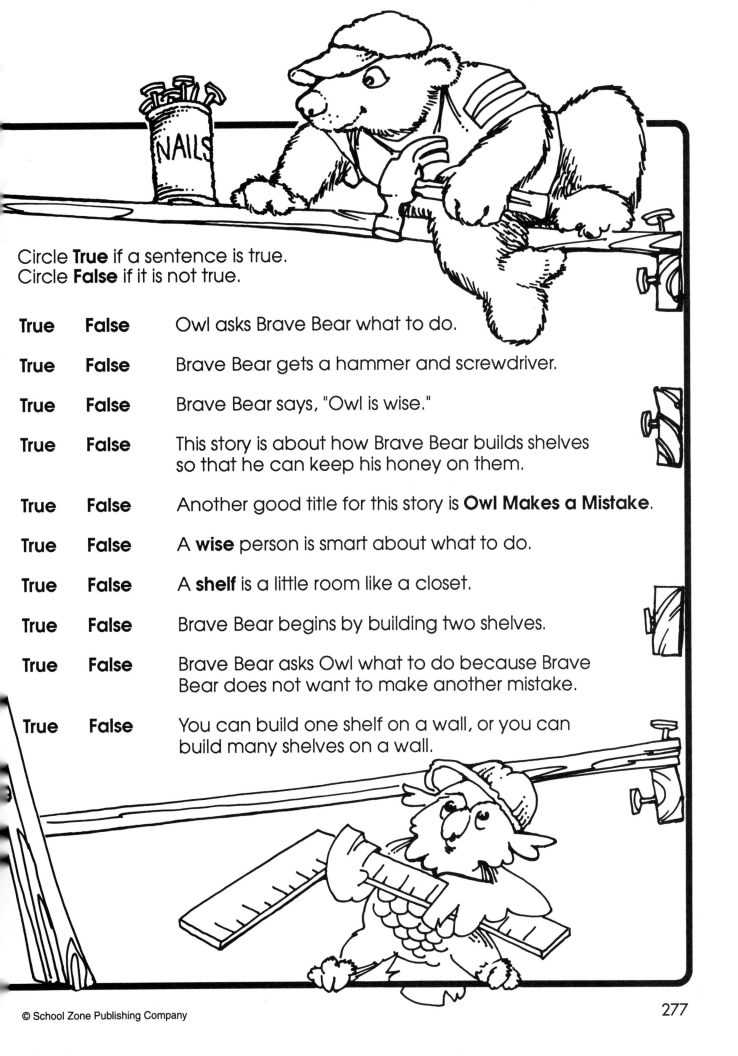

Circle **True** if a sentence is true.
Circle **False** if it is not true.

True   **False**   Owl asks Brave Bear what to do.

True   **False**   Brave Bear gets a hammer and screwdriver.

True   **False**   Brave Bear says, "Owl is wise."

True   **False**   This story is about how Brave Bear builds shelves so that he can keep his honey on them.

True   **False**   Another good title for this story is **Owl Makes a Mistake**.

True   **False**   A **wise** person is smart about what to do.

True   **False**   A **shelf** is a little room like a closet.

True   **False**   Brave Bear begins by building two shelves.

True   **False**   Brave Bear asks Owl what to do because Brave Bear does not want to make another mistake.

True   **False**   You can build one shelf on a wall, or you can build many shelves on a wall.

Name That Finger

Each finger of your hand has a name. It's not a name like Suzie or Chad or Larry. It's a name like *thumb*.

Yes, thumb is the name of one of the five fingers. The thumb is the finger that sticks out to the side. You can touch each of your other four fingers with your thumb. That's because the thumb moves in a different direction.

The finger next to the thumb is called the index finger. You use this finger to flip through a pile of papers one at a time.

After that comes the middle finger. There are two fingers before it and two after it. This is why it's called the middle finger.

Next to the middle finger is the ring finger. It is called the ring finger because people often wear a ring on this finger.

The last finger has two names. Some people call it the little finger. Other people call it the pinkie.

Look at the numbers on the drawing.
Read each question and circle the correct answer.

What is the name of finger number 3?
      ring   **middle**   **index**

What is the name of finger number 5?
      tiny   **thumb**   **pinkie**

What is the name of finger number 2?
      middle   **index**   **little**

What is the name of finger number 4?
      ring   **index**   **pinkie**

Which animal has hands like ours?
      frog   **monkey**   **dog**

Brave Bear Sorts Honey

Brave Bear was very happy with his new shelves. "I will put my honey on the shelves," he said.

Brave Bear looked around. He had many, many jars of honey. Some jars were full of dark-colored honey. Sage honey was dark. And buckwheat was dark. "I love dark honey," said Brave Bear, licking his lips. "It tastes so sweet!"

More of the jars were full of light-colored honey. Clover honey was light. Linden honey was also light. So was orange honey. And lavender honey was also light in color. "I love light honey," said Brave Bear, opening a jar. "It tastes so sweet!"

Brave Bear ate some honey and looked at the jars. "I must sort these jars," he said. "I must have a plan."

Brave Bear thought about it. "I know," he said. "I will put all my dark honey on the left-hand shelves. And I will put all my light honey on the right-hand shelves." And so he did.

Write the names of the dark honey on the **left**.
Write the names of the light honey on the **right**.

orange   buckwheat   clover   linden   sage   lavender

Dark Honey	Light Honey
_____	_____
_____	_____
	_____
	_____

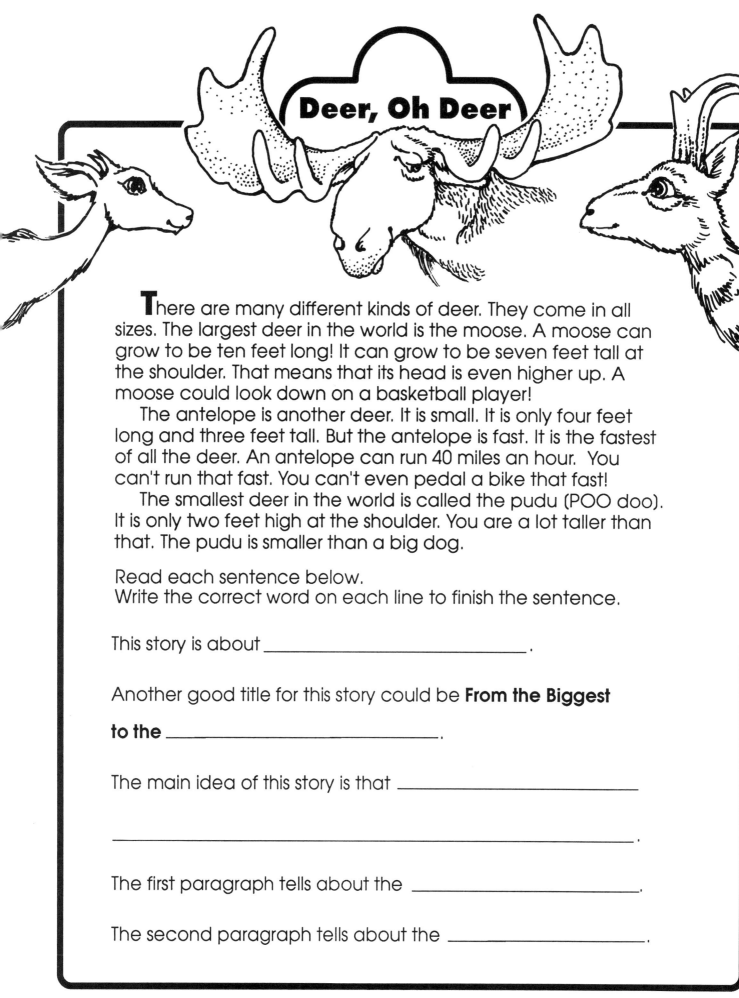

Deer, Oh Deer

There are many different kinds of deer. They come in all sizes. The largest deer in the world is the moose. A moose can grow to be ten feet long! It can grow to be seven feet tall at the shoulder. That means that its head is even higher up. A moose could look down on a basketball player!

The antelope is another deer. It is small. It is only four feet long and three feet tall. But the antelope is fast. It is the fastest of all the deer. An antelope can run 40 miles an hour. You can't run that fast. You can't even pedal a bike that fast!

The smallest deer in the world is called the pudu (POO doo). It is only two feet high at the shoulder. You are a lot taller than that. The pudu is smaller than a big dog.

Read each sentence below.
Write the correct word on each line to finish the sentence.

This story is about _____.

Another good title for this story could be **From the Biggest**

to the _____.

The main idea of this story is that _____

_____.

The first paragraph tells about the _____.

The second paragraph tells about the _____.

280

Greenland Is Not Green

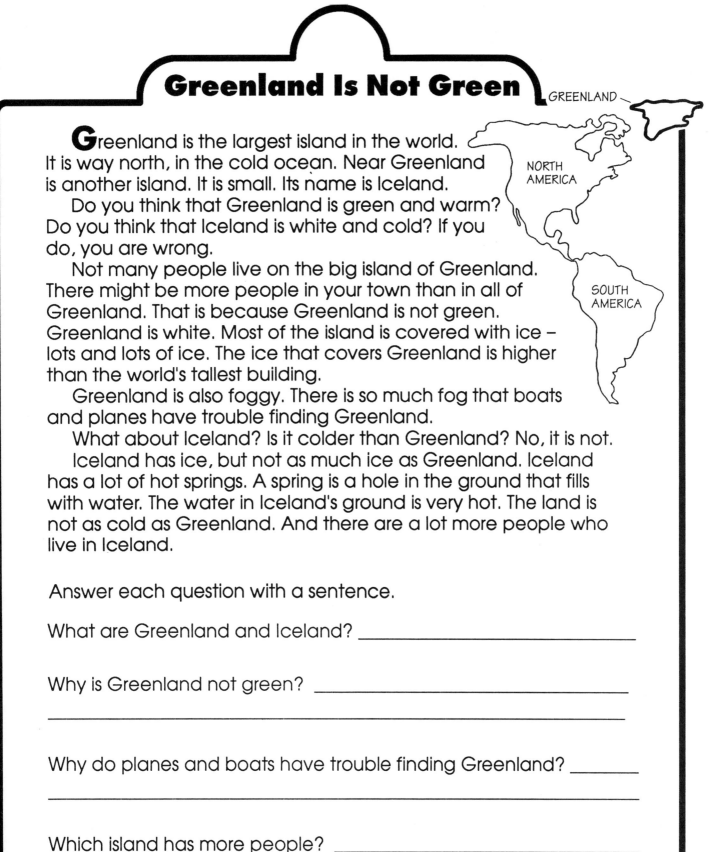

GREENLAND

NORTH AMERICA

SOUTH AMERICA

Greenland is the largest island in the world. It is way north, in the cold ocean. Near Greenland is another island. It is small. Its name is Iceland.

Do you think that Greenland is green and warm? Do you think that Iceland is white and cold? If you do, you are wrong.

Not many people live on the big island of Greenland. There might be more people in your town than in all of Greenland. That is because Greenland is not green. Greenland is white. Most of the island is covered with ice – lots and lots of ice. The ice that covers Greenland is higher than the world's tallest building.

Greenland is also foggy. There is so much fog that boats and planes have trouble finding Greenland.

What about Iceland? Is it colder than Greenland? No, it is not.

Iceland has ice, but not as much ice as Greenland. Iceland has a lot of hot springs. A spring is a hole in the ground that fills with water. The water in Iceland's ground is very hot. The land is not as cold as Greenland. And there are a lot more people who live in Iceland.

Answer each question with a sentence.

What are Greenland and Iceland? _____

Why is Greenland not green? _____
_____

Why do planes and boats have trouble finding Greenland? _____
_____

Which island has more people? _____

Why do more people live on the smaller island? _____
_____

Penguins

Penguins are black and white birds. Penguins do not stand like other birds. They stand up straight, like a person does. When they walk, they walk very, very slowly.

They have wings, but penguins do not use their wings to fly. Penguins cannot fly. Instead, they swim. They use their wings like flippers. They use them to move in the water. When penguins swim, they swim very fast. Of all the birds that swim underwater, penguins swim the fastest.

Penguins can walk, and penguins can swim. There is one other way that penguins can move. If it wants to go down a hill, a penguin gets on its belly. Then it slides down the hill. That is much faster than walking.

Read each sentence below.
Write the correct word on each line to finish the sentence.

This story is about _____.

Another good title for this story could be

How _____ **Move**.

The main idea of this story is that _____

_____.

The second paragraph tells how penguins _____.

The third paragraph tells how penguins _____.

The Olympics

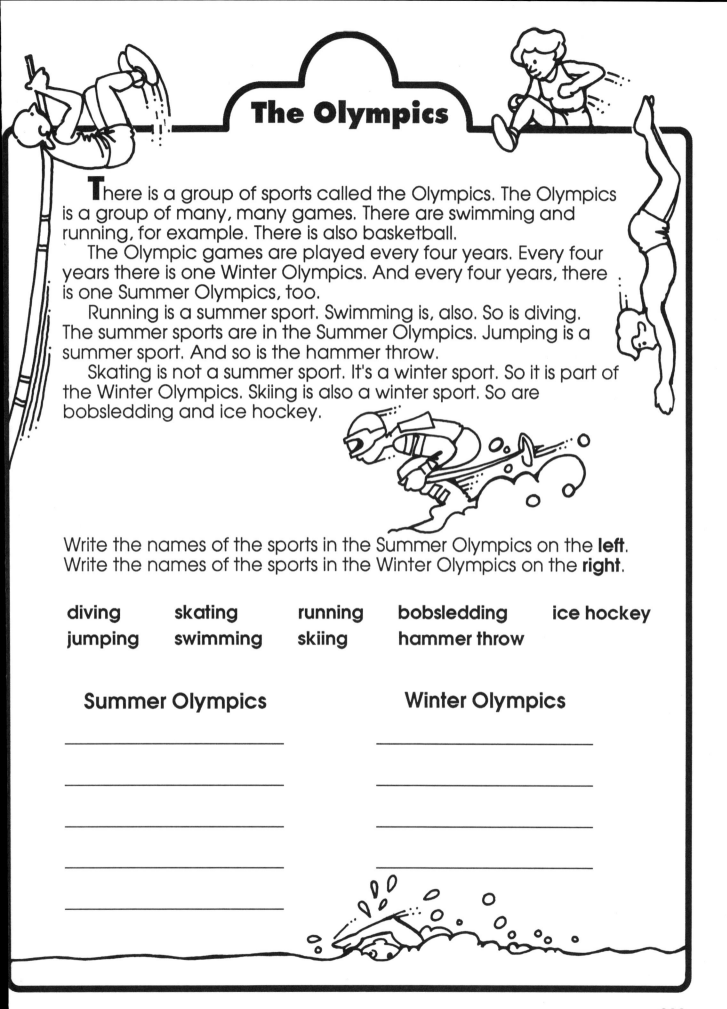

There is a group of sports called the Olympics. The Olympics is a group of many, many games. There are swimming and running, for example. There is also basketball.

The Olympic games are played every four years. Every four years there is one Winter Olympics. And every four years, there is one Summer Olympics, too.

Running is a summer sport. Swimming is, also. So is diving. The summer sports are in the Summer Olympics. Jumping is a summer sport. And so is the hammer throw.

Skating is not a summer sport. It's a winter sport. So it is part of the Winter Olympics. Skiing is also a winter sport. So are bobsledding and ice hockey.

Write the names of the sports in the Summer Olympics on the **left**.
Write the names of the sports in the Winter Olympics on the **right**.

| diving | skating | running | bobsledding | ice hockey |
| jumping | swimming | skiing | hammer throw | |

Summer Olympics   **Winter Olympics**

_____   _____

_____   _____

_____   _____

_____   _____

_____

Brave Bear walked through the woods. Way up in the sky, he could see the sun. It was way above the tree tops. But down here in the forest, it was dark and cool.

Up ahead was a berry bush. Brave Bear smelled the bush. Yum. He sat down in front of the bush. He ate the berries, every last one of them. "Those were good berries," said Brave Bear.

Brave Bear came to the river. He drank some water. The cold water tasted good. Then Brave Bear jumped into the river. The cold water felt good. He swam and swam. He even ate a few fish.

After he got out of the river, Brave Bear walked up a hill. He saw a bee. "If I follow the bee," said Brave Bear, "I will find honey." So he followed the bee and found the beehive. Of course Brave Bear ate the honey.

"I am tired," said Brave Bear. "I will take a nap." So he found a soft spot beside a log. He curled up. And he took a long nap.

Write a sentence to answer each question.

Why is it dark and cool in the forest? _____

_____

Why did Brave Bear follow the bee? _____

_____

Why was it a good idea for Brave Bear to follow the bee?

_____

What would it be like to be a bear for one day?

_____

_____

They Go Together

A pair is two things that go together. A salt shaker and pepper shaker are a pair. A left shoe and a right shoe are also a pair.

People can also be a pair. A mother and father are a pair. Two brothers are a pair. Two sisters are a pair. A brother and a sister are also a pair. Batman and Robin are a pair.

Can you think of some famous pairs in stories? These are people or animals who go together. Think of a brother and sister in a forest. That pair is Hansel and Gretel. Think of two children who go up a hill. Who is the pair? It's Jack and Jill, of course.

Now think about cartoons. Who are the squirrel and the moose that make a pair? It's Rocky and Bullwinkle. A little bear and a big bear live in Jellystone Park. Who is this famous pair? It's Boo Boo and Yogi Bear.

There are many famous pairs. How many can you think of?

Circle **True** if a sentence is most likely true.
Circle **False** if it is most likely false.
Write sentences to answer the last two questions.

True   **False**   Only real live people can be pairs.

True   **False**   Superman and Lois Lane are a pair.

True   **False**   A man and a salt shaker are a pair.

Name two things that are **not** a pair. _____

Name some pairs that aren't in the story. _____

_____

285

Brave Bear Teaches

Owl was teaching the animals about other animals. "I will teach you about the dog family," said Owl.

"There are many animals in the dog family. First, there is the wolf. It belongs to the dog family. Then there is the coyote. It also belongs. And so does the fox."

"That is nice," said Brave Bear.

Owl said, "There is the jackal. The jackal belongs to the dog family. And of course, there is the dog. It belongs to the dog family."

Owl looked at Brave Bear. "I wonder," said Owl, "if the bear belongs to the dog family. Is the bear just a large dog without a tail?"

Brave Bear stood up. "No!" he shouted. "The bear is not a dog! Bears belong to the bear family!"

"The brown bear belongs to this family. So does the black bear. And so does the polar bear." Brave Bear was not done. "The sun bear belongs to the bear family. So does the sloth bear. Bears are bears," said Brave Bear. "We are not dogs."

Write the names of the animals in the **Dog Family** on the **left**.
Write the names of the animals in the **Bear Family** on the **right**.

| sun | wolf | jackal | sloth | brown |
| fox | black | coyote | polar | dog |

Dog Family   Bear Family

_____   _____

_____   _____

_____   _____

_____   _____

Page 257
house
door
bed
pet
honey

Page 258
Rabbit
sound
ears
Mother

Page 259
trees
there are many different
kinds of trees.
Trees
leaves
biggest

Page 260
bedroom
yes
Owl
space
honey

Page 261
log
bone
luck
jog
truck

Page 262
plant
cornmeal
yellow
cob
pop

Page 263
e
d
a
c
b

Page 264
stilts
people use stilts
for work or play.
Tall
tall/ long/ high
shelf

Page 265
blocks
better
box
door
you

Pages 266 & 267
False
True
True
False
True
False
True
False
False
True

Page 268
sea
head
shellfish
They squirt ink.
It can squeeze into cracks.

Page 269
b
a
d
e
c

Pages 270 & 271
Rabbit has taken Brave Bear's blue boat.
His boat has honey in the front.
The boats looked alike.
He does not know the rest of the words.
The boat with carrots is his boat.
Rabbit is in his own boat.

Page 272
Otters live on land and water.
It is snow.
Their mothers teach young animals what to do.
She slides down a hill in the snow.
Tall animals would have a hard time bending
close to the ground.

Page 273
money/trade
Use money to buy things.
Money/Trading
trade
Money is easy to carry and use.

Page 274
It spins around in space.
It comes very close to Earth
and begins to fall.
It falls through the air.
It burns.

Page 275
False
False
True
False
Tanya is pulling a
joke on Richard.

Pages 276 & 277
False
False
True
True
False
True
False
False
True
True

Page 278
middle
pinkie
index
ring
monkey

Page 279
Dark Honey
sage
buckwheat

Light Honey
orange
clover
linden
lavender

Page 280
deer
Smallest or Littlest
There are many different kinds of deer.
moose
antelope

Page 281
They are islands.
It is covered with ice.
There is fog all around it.
Iceland has more people.
More people live on Iceland
because it is warmer than
Greenland.

Page 282
penguins
Penguins
penguins move
in three ways.
swim
slide

Page 283
Summer Olympics
diving
running
jumping
swimming
hammer throw

Winter Olympics
skating
bobsledding
ice hockey
skiing

Page 284
It is dark and cool in the forest because the trees keep out most of the sun.
Brave Bear follows the bee so that the bee will lead him to honey.
It is a good idea for Brave Bear to follow the bee because the bee leads him to honey.
Answers will vary.

Page 285
False
True
False
Answers will vary.
Answers will vary.

Page 286
Dog Family	Bear Family
wolf	sun
jackal	sloth
fox	brown
coyote	black
dog	polar

BEGINNING CONSONANTS

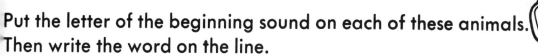

Put the letter of the beginning sound on each of these animals.
Then write the word on the line.

___ightingale _____

___ear _____

___ig _____

___at _____

___uail _____

___og _____

___abbit _____

___ish _____

___eal _____

___oat _____

___iger _____

___orse _____

___ulture _____

___aguar _____

___alrus _____

___angaroo_____

fo___ _____

___ion _____

___ak _____

___ouse _____

___ebra_____

SHORT "A" WORDS

Read the short "a" words in the apple.
Then do what each sentence tells you.

at as
cat fan am
ant an had

1. Write the spelling words that have two letters.

_____ _____ _____ _____

2. Write the spelling words that have three letters.

_____ _____ _____ _____

Make new words. Trace over the beginning letter.
Write the short "a" family after it. Now say the word.

at	am	an	ad
b	h	r	b
h	S	m	d
m	r	t	h
p	j	p	m
s	d	f	l

290

SHORT "E" WORDS

Answer the riddles. Use one word from the short "e" list.
Write the word on the line.

tent

sled

hen

pen

cent

bell

belt

bed

nest

leg

desk

ten

1. You ride on me in winter. _____

2. Write with me. _____

3. Sleep in me outdoors. _____

4. I can ring. _____

5. Hop on me. _____

6. I come after nine. _____

7. I lay eggs. _____

8. Put papers on me. _____

9. I hold up your pants. _____

My name is Fred. Does that mean that I'm a short "e" word?

10. Dream on me. _____

11. Ten of me make a dime. _____

12. Baby birds grow in me. _____

SHORT "I" WORDS

Fill in the blanks with "i" to make silly sentences.
Read the sentences to a friend.

1. I h__d the l__d, I d__d.
2. I w__ll f__ll the p__ll with d__ll.
3. The w__tch fell in the d__tch with her sw__tch.
4. I w__sh the f__sh were st__ll in the d__sh.
5. Please l__ft the g__ft over the r__ft.
6. "You're a p__p," said the l__p to the h__p as
   they took a s__p.
7. The b__g p__g had on a w__g as he ate a f__g.
8. He l__t up the p__t to make __t f__t to s__t __n.

Add the beginning letter to make the same words that are
in the sentences above.

___id	___ill	___ish	___it
___id	___ill	___ish	___it
___id	___ill	___ish	___it
	___ill		___it

SHORT "O" WORDS

Add an "o" to these letters to make words.
Write the word in the blank space.

b__p _____   d__ck _____   c__t _____
c__p _____   l__ck _____   d__t _____
h__p _____   m__ck _____   g__t _____
m__p _____   r__ck _____   h__t _____
p__p _____   s__ck _____   l__t _____
t__p _____   t__ck _____   p__t _____

SILLY SENTENCES

Add an "o" to make short vowel words.

1. The c__p put the m__p on t__p of P__p!
2. I g__t a r__ck in my s__ck at the d__ck.
3. I have n__t g__t a h__t p__t on my c__t.

SHORT "U" WORDS

Read the short "u" words inside the umbrella.

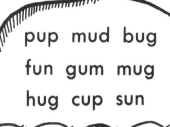

pup mud bug
fun gum mug
hug cup sun

Write two pairs that rhyme.

_____   _____

_____   _____

Write the beginning letter for each picture to make a word.

1. _____

2. _____

3. _____

4. _____

5. _____

6. _____

7. _____

8. _____

9. _____

Running in the sun is fun!

SHORT VOWEL REVIEW

Add the right vowel to make a word.
Copy the words on the lines next to the correct vowel.

A
_____
_____
_____

E
_____
_____

I
_____
_____

O
_____
_____
_____

U
_____
_____

p___n
c___t

d___g   h___t

p___g
h___t

h___n
r___d

b___s

b___nd
b___ck

n___t

t___b

g___m

l___g
b___d

h___ll
s___ck

t___p
p___p

LONG "A" WORDS

When an "a" is followed by a "y" or an "i," it says its own name.

Using the words in the snail, help her get to the pail by writing the words on the line.

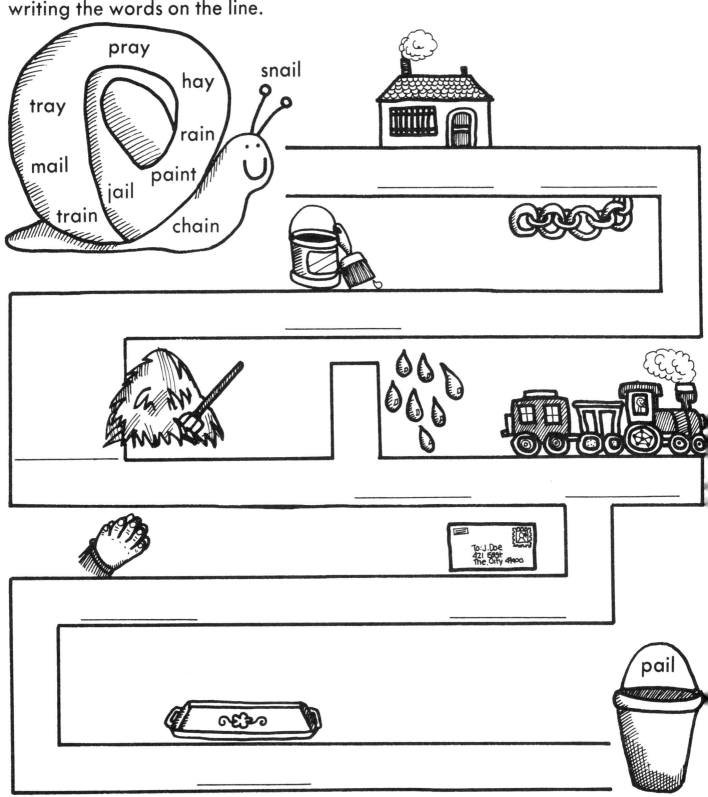

THE MAGIC "E"

Add "e" to the word and make a new word with a long vowel sound.

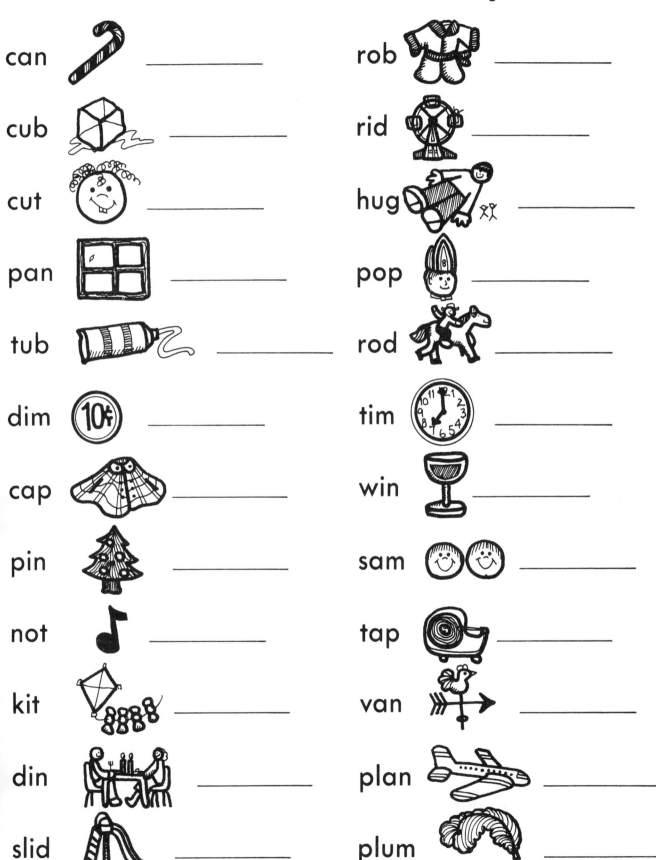

can _____

cub _____

cut _____

pan _____

tub _____

dim _____

cap _____

pin _____

not _____

kit _____

din _____

slid _____

rob _____

rid _____

hug _____

pop _____

rod _____

tim _____

win _____

sam _____

tap _____

van _____

plan _____

plum _____

LONG "E" WORDS

Long "e" sounds are made by "ea," "ee," or "ey." Color the long "e" words grey to make a picture.

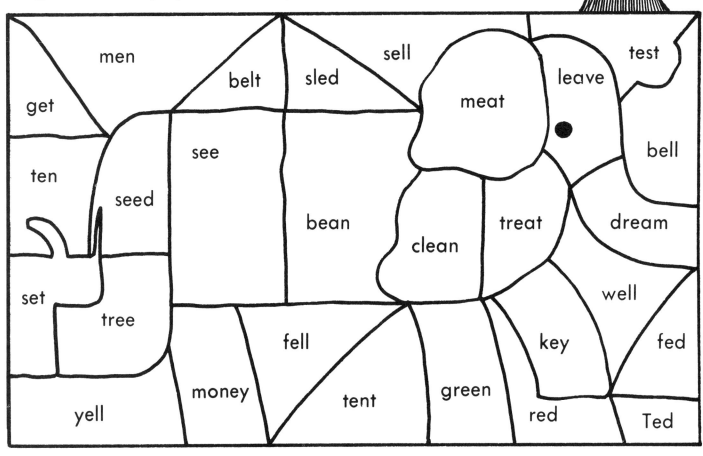

men
get
ten
set
seed
tree
yell
belt
see
money
sled
bean
fell
sell
meat
clean
tent
treat
green
leave
test
bell
dream
well
key
red
fed
Ted

Write the long "e" words on the lines below.

_____ _____

_____ _____

_____ _____

_____ _____

_____ _____

This is the greenest bean I've ever seen!

298

LONG "I" WORDS

The sound of "i" can be in a word as "ie" or "igh."
Sometimes a "y" sounds like "i."

Color the long "i" words in red and those that are not long "i" in blue.

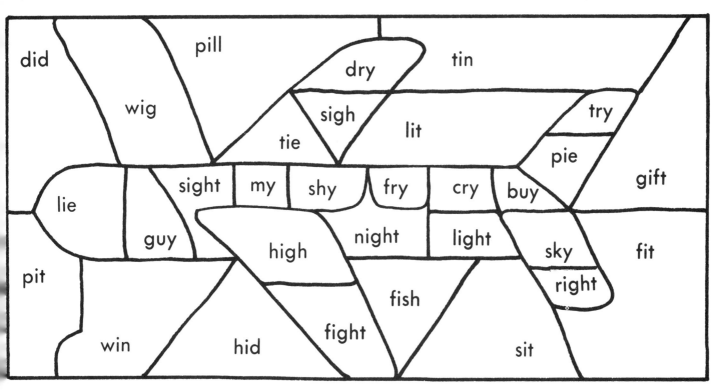

did
pill
dry
tin
wig
sigh
lit
try
tie
pie
sight   my   shy   fry   cry   buy
gift
lie
night   light
guy
high
sky
fit
right
pit
fish
win   hid   fight   sit

Write the long "i" words on the lines below.

uy	ie	igh

_____   _____   _____   _____

_____   _____ | y | _____

_____   _____   _____

LONG "O" WORDS

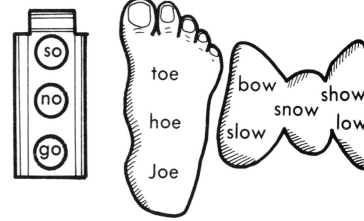

List the two letter words.

_____

_____

_____

List the three letter words.

_____   _____

_____   _____

List all the "oa" words.

_____

_____

_____

List all the "ow" words.

_____

_____

_____

300

LONG "U" WORDS

U-E

In order to say its name, "u" likes an "e" on the end.

h__ge _____   r__de _____

c__be _____   t__ne _____

d__ne _____   c__te _____

t__be _____   f__me _____

U-I

It likes to be with "i" as in:

fr__ __t _____   j__ __ce _____   s__ __t _____

But "q" never goes without "u." Try these words.

q__eer _____   sq__ash _____

q__ick _____   sq__eal _____

q__ake _____   sq__eak _____

q__ilt _____   sq__ish _____

q__ack _____   sq__int _____

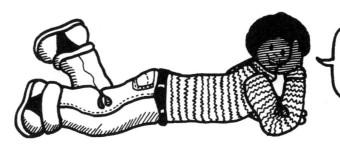

I don't mean to be rude, but I could really use a rest!

BE SMART

MAKE WORDS USING THESE ENDINGS

old

b _____

c _____

f _____

h _____

m _____

s _____

t _____

ink

l _____

m _____

r _____

s _____

w _____

p _____

th _____

bl _____

ing

k _____

r _____

s _____

w _____

cl _____

br _____

str _____

fl _____

spr _____

th _____

ang

b _____

f _____

h _____

r _____

s _____

ake

b _____

c _____

f _____

J _____

l _____

m _____

r _____

s _____

t _____

w _____

fl _____

br _____

st _____

ate

d _____

f _____

h _____

l _____

m _____

r _____

pl _____

cr _____

sk _____

ank

b _____

d _____

l _____

r _____

s _____

fr _____

sp _____

bl _____

th _____

cr _____

dr _____

ick

D _____

h _____

l _____

p _____

s _____

t _____

w _____

cl _____

sl _____

br _____

tr _____

st _____

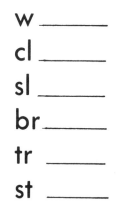

Look at all these new words you made!

THE "L" BLENDS

"L" likes to be next to these consonants.

Make words using these "l" blends. Fill in the blanks.
Then write the words on the line. Say the words.

bl
_____ock _____
_____ess _____
_____ink _____
_____ow _____

gl
_____ad _____
_____ass _____
_____obe _____
_____itter _____

cl
_____own _____
_____ock _____
_____ub _____
_____ass _____

pl
_____an _____
_____ay _____
_____us _____
_____ant _____

fl
_____ower _____
_____ag _____
_____y _____
_____ash _____

sl
_____ip _____
_____eep _____
_____im _____
_____acks _____

THE "S" BLENDS

Draw a line under two endings that make a word using the beginning letters. Say the words. The first one is done for you.

sk	spr	scr
ock	ot	ing
ime	ay	am
<u>ate</u>	ing	eam
<u>in</u>	ub	ank

sp	sc	squ
eed	alp	ish
ash	est	am
ill	ale	eak
one	art	ay

st	str	spl
ing	ike	it
amp	ame	ing
ike	og	ash
ame	eet	ug

sl	sn	sh
eep	ess	ang
ak	ap	eet
aunt	ail	unk
am	eat	ame

sm	sw	shr
oke	ip	one
ick	oan	en
ell	eet	ink
one	im	ub

THE "R" BLENDS

Color the "r" blends green to make a picture.

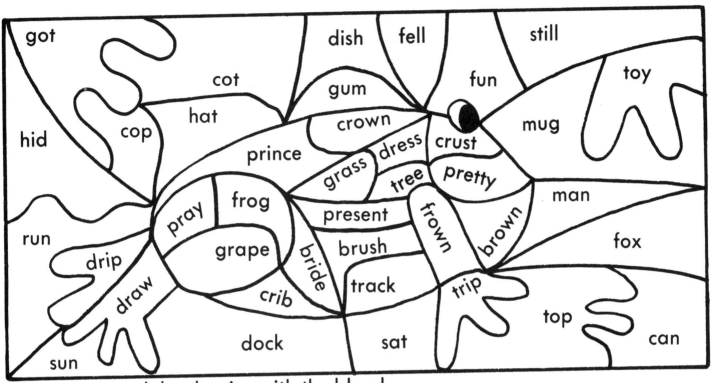

Write one word that begins with the blend.

br _____

fr _____

pr _____

cr _____

gr _____

tr _____

dr _____

BLENDS REVIEW

Make a new word by adding the ending to the blend.
Say the words. The first one is done for you.

gray   **pr**ay

cry   **fr**_____

crash   **tr**_____

drip   **fl**_____

grow   **bl**_____

block   **cr**_____

brown   **dr**_____

skill   **sp**_____

brush   **bl**_____

crack   **tr**_____

bring   **cl**_____

frog   **sm**_____

tr_____

fl_____

cl_____

sl_____

cr_____

cl_____

fr_____

st_____

cr_____

bl_____

fl_____

cl_____

pl_____

sk_____

sm_____

sk_____

sl_____

sm_____

cl_____

gr_____

pl_____

st_____

st_____

fl_____

That wasn't bad at all, was it?

SH CH TH WH

Some letters make a new sound when they're put together. Do these letters go at the beginning or at the end ?

Write the word on the line.

sh	**ch**	**th**	**wh**
ake _shake_	in _chin_	ink _think_	eat _wheat_
wa _____	por _____	ird _____	eel _____
op _____	ild _____	mou _____	ale _____
ed _____	ea _____	umb _____	ip _____
fi _____	ri _____	ba _____	istle _____
ade _____	in _____	clo _____	y _____
ell _____	su _____	bo _____	ich _____
irt _____	whi _____	wor _____	at _____
fre _____	erry _____	sou _____	ile _____
ca _____	wat _____	pa _____	ite _____
eep _____	air _____	ick _____	isker _____
ip _____	eese _____	nor _____	ere _____

HELP THE BOY

The sound of "oi" in oil and "oy" in boy is the same.

Write an "oi" or an "oy" in each word to go through the path to the toy plane.

b__ __   p__ __nt   br__ __l

v__ __d   sp__ __l   c__ __   s__ __l   n__ __se

m__ __st   h__ __st   __ __l   ch__ __ce

j__ __n   j__ __   c__ __n

b__ __l   v__ __ce   t__ __

RIDDLES

Some words have the same vowel sound, but it's made with different letters.

moon   **suit**   **glue**   **blew**

Answer the riddles using words from the list. Write the word on the line.

moose
blue
pew
dew
broom
tooth
true
chew
pool
stool
glue
school

1. The color of the sky. _____

2. You find me on the grass in the morning. _____

3. Stick things together with me. _____

4. A big animal with antlers. _____

5. The name of a seat in church. _____

6. What you do with gum. _____

7. You can sit on me. _____

8. Sweep the floor with me. _____

9. The opposite of false. _____

10. Brush me twice a day. _____

11. This is where you learn every day. _____

12. You can swim in me. _____

SILLY SENTENCES

The sound of "ou" as in mouse and "ow" as in owl are the same.

Fill in the blanks with "ou" or "ow."

1. A Boy Sc __ __ t will not p __ __ t or fr __ __ n.

2. The br __ __ n tr __ __ t cannot dr __ __ n in water.

3. The h __ __ nd said " __ __ ch" with a l __ __ d h __ __ l!

4. The cl __ __ n sat d __ __ n ar __ __ nd the fl __ __ ers.

5. C __ __ nt the cr __ __ d d __ __ n at the r __ __ nd t __ __ er.

6. The cr __ __ n is h __ __ the king ann __ __ nces his p __ __ er.

7. My m __ __ th has a s __ __ r taste.

8. I f __ __ nd a m __ __ se in my h __ __ se under the c __ __ ch.

Write 4 "ou" words.

_____

_____

_____

_____

Write 4 "ow" words.

_____

_____

_____

_____

SILENT LETTERS

Quiet Zone

Sometimes the letters l, k, w, h, t, b, and gh are silent.
Add the silent letters, then write the word on the line.

 w

__ rap _____

__ rong _____

__ rite _____

 gh

hi __ __ _____

nau __ __ ty _____

ni __ __ t _____

 b

dum __ _____

thum __ _____

crum __ _____

t

ca __ ch _____

ma __ ch _____

wi __ ch _____

k

__ nob _____

__ nit _____

__ nee _____

 l

wa __ k _____

sta __ k _____

ta __ k _____

 h

__ onest _____

__ our _____

g __ ost _____

shhhhhh!

See if you can still find the word when they're mixed up.

cha __ k _____

__ nock _____

__ now _____

fi __ __ t _____

com __ _____

ca __ f _____

__ new _____

lam __ _____

__ rite _____

ki __ chen _____

scra __ ch _____

ri __ __ t _____

"R" MAKES IT DIFFERENT

Whenever an "r" comes next to a vowel, it makes the sound different. Put either <u>ar</u>, <u>er</u>, <u>ir</u>, <u>or</u>, or <u>ur</u> in the blanks to make a story. Check your answers to make sure they're correct.

A g__ __l with a c__ __l on h__ __ f__ __ehead was going to the p__ __k. She took h__ __ p__ __se and w__ __e sh__ __ts and a sh__ __t. When she left her front p__ __ch, a man in a d__ __k c__ __ blew his h__ __n. It was h__ __ fath__ __. He thought his daught__ __ was v__ __y sm__ __t and ch__ __ming.

At the p__ __k there was a b__ __n with f__ __m animals in it. Fath__ __ let h__ __ ride a h__ __se. She fell off and was h__ __t. A n__ __se fixed her __ __m. Fath__ __ and daught__ __ then went to the p__ __k st__ __e and bought some popc__ __n. She was th__ __sty so she had an __ __ange drink.

When they got home, Moth__ __ had a b__ __thday p__ __ty f__ __ h__ __. It was a wond__ __ful b__ __thday!

C AND G

I sound like "k" before these letters.

A O U

I sound like "s" before these letters.

I E Y

Copy the words. Say them as you write.

cat	_____	city	_____
cot	_____	cigar	_____
candy	_____	lace	_____
coffee	_____	face	_____
could	_____	ice	_____
cup	_____	cycle	_____

Then there's circus _____.

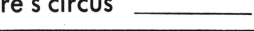

I sound like the "g" in goat before these letters.

A O U

I usually sound like "j" before these letters.

I E Y

Copy the words. Say them as you write.

gas	_____	gym	_____
gum	_____	gem	_____
go	_____	magic	_____
good	_____	gentle	_____
get	_____	large	_____
gull	_____	page	_____

Then there's garbage _____.

USE AN APOSTROPHE TO MAKE WORDS SMALLER

Match the two words with the short one.   Write the contraction on the line.
The first one is done for you.

are not	I'll	aren't
you will	can't	_____
they are	aren't	_____
I have	they're	_____
can not	you'll	_____
he is	I've	_____
could not	we've	_____
I will	he's	_____
we have	couldn't	_____
is not	we're	_____
did not	they'll	_____
they will	isn't	_____
we are	didn't	_____

How did you do on this page?

MAKE ONE WORD OUT OF TWO

dog house

doghouse

Look at the pictures. Then write the compound word on the line.

foot + ball	_____
light + house	_____
rain + bow	_____
fire + man	_____
door + bell	_____
cup + cake	_____
star + fish	_____
cow + boy	_____
bird + house	_____
wrist + watch / dog	_____
step + ladder	_____
ear + drum	_____
tooth + brush	_____

HOW DO YOU HANDLE MORE THAN ONE?

Sometimes you add "s." Write the word, adding "s."

book _____   clock _____   mother _____

hand _____   flower _____   doll _____

When the word ends in "x," "ss," "ch," or "sh," you add "es."

box _____   witch _____   dish _____

dress _____   wish _____   church _____

When the word ends in "y," usually you change the "y" to "i" and add "es."

baby _____   pony _____   fairy _____

penny _____   berry _____   city _____

When the word ends in "f," you change the "f" to "v" and add "es."

leaf _____   wife _____   knife _____

Our teacher knows how to handle more than one!

316

ENDINGS ARE DIFFERENT

Do what it tells you.

Use a double consonant before adding "ing" when a verb ends in a consonant preceded by a single vowel.

Just add "ing."	Drop "e" and add "ing."	
think _____	love _____	run _____
sing _____	save _____	swim _____
work _____	make _____	jog _____
yell _____	come _____	step _____

Sometimes you just add a suffix.

Add "ful."	Add "er" or "est."	Add "ness" or "less."
wonder _____	small _____	sick _____
care _____	fast _____	good _____
cup _____	slow _____	care _____
thank _____	old _____	hard _____
help _____	hard _____	kind _____
pain _____	kind _____	help _____

Hmmmm... endings ARE different!

BEGINNINGS
MAKE A DIFFERENCE

Do the word puzzle.

"Un" in front of a word means "not."

u	n					
u	n				
u	n				
u	n				
u	n				
u	n				

1. not happy
2. not able
3. not safe
4. not kind
5. not even
6. not tied

"Mis" in front of a word means "wrong."

m	i	s				
m	i	s					
m	i	s				
m	i	s				
m	i	s				
m	i	s			

1. wrong fit
2. wrong place
3. wrong deal
4. wrong fire
5. wrong count
6. wrong spell

Page 289

bear
cat
dog
fish
goat
horse
jaguar
kangaroo
lion
mouse
nightingale
pig
quail
rabbit
seal
tiger
vulture
walrus
fox
yak
zebra

Page 290

1. at, as, an am
2. fan, had, ant, cat

bat	ham	ran	bad
hat	Sam	man	dad
mat	ram	tan	had
pat	jam	pan	mad
sat	dam	fan	lad

Page 291

1. sled
2. pen
3. tent
4. bell
5. leg
6. ten
7. hen
8. desk
9. belt
10. bed
11. cent
12. nest

Page 292

1. I hid the lid, I did.
2. I will fill the pill with dill.
3. The witch fell in the ditch with her switch.
4. I wish the fish were still in the dish.
5. Please lift the gift over the rift.
6. "You're a pip," said the lip to the hip as they took a sip.
7. The big pig had on a wig as he ate a fig.
8. He lit up the pit to make it fit to sit in.

hid	will	wish	lit
lid	fill	fish	pit
did	pill	dish	fit
	dill		sit

Page 293

1. The cop put the mop on top of Pop!
2. I got a rock in my sock at the dock.
3. I have not got a hot pot on my cot.

Page 294

pup, cup
bug, mug, hug
fun, sun

1. pup
2. gum
3. mug
4. fun
5. hug
6. bug
7. cup
8. sun
9. mud

Page 295

A	I	U
pan	pig	bus
cat	hit	gum
band	hill	nut
back	sick	tub

E	O
hen	dog
red	hot
bed	top
leg	pop

Page 296

jail
chain
paint
hay
rain
train
mail
pray
tray

Page 297

Automatic fill in.

Page 298

meat
clean
leave
green
money
bean
seed
see
key
treat
tree
dream

Page 299

uy	y
guy	my
buy	shy
	try
igh	fry
high	sky
night	dry
light	cry
fight	
sight	**ie**
sigh	lie
right	pie
	tie

Page 300

Two letter
so
no
go
Three letter
toe
hoe
Joe
low
bow

ow
slow
bow
snow
show
low

oa
toast
road
boat
goat
toad
soap

Page 301

Automatic fill in.

Page 302

Automatic fill in.

Page 303

Automatic fill in.

Page 304

skate	spray	scram
skin	spring	scream
speed	scalp	squish
spill	scale	squeak
sting	strike	split
stamp	street	splash
sleep	snap	sheet
slam	snail	shame
smoke	sweet	shrink
smell	swim	shrub

Page 305

br	tr	pr
brown	trip	pretty
bride	tree	pray
brush	track	prince
		present

dr	cr
drip	crib
draw	crust
dress	crown

gr	fr
grape	frown
grass	frog

Page 306

Automatic fill in.

Page 307

sh	ch	th	wh
wash	porch	third	wheel
shop	child	mouth	whale
shed	each	thumb	whip
fish	rich	bath	whistle
shade	chin or inch	cloth	why
shell	such	both	which
shirt	which	worth	what
fresh	cherry	south	while
cash	watch	path	white
sheep	chair	thick	whisker
ship	cheese	north	where

Page 308

boy	hoist
point	oil
broil	choice
noise	coin
soil	joy
coy	join
spoil	boil
void	voice
moist	toy

Page 309

1. blue
2. dew
3. glue
4. moose
5. pew
6. chew
7. stool
8. broom
9. true
10. tooth
11. school
12. pool

Page 310

1. A Boy Scout will not pout or frown.
2. The brown trout cannot drown in water.
3. The hound said "Ouch" with a loud howl!
4. The clown sat down around the flowers.
5. Count the crowd down at the round tower.
6. The crown is how the king announces his power.
7. My mouth has a sour taste
8. I found a mouse in my house under the couch.

Scout	house	frown	crown
pout	couch	brown	how
trout	around	drown	power
hound	count	howl	down
loud	sour	clown	
ouch	mouth	flowers	
announces	mouse	crowd	
found		tower	

Page 311

Automatic fill in.

chalk
knock
know
fight

comb
calf
knew
lamb

write
kitchen
scratch
right

Page 312

A girl with a curl on her forehead was going to the park. She took her purse and wore shorts and a shirt. When she left her front porch, a man in a dark car blew his horn. It was her father. He thought his daughter was very smart and charming.

At the park there was a barn with farm animals in it. Father let her ride a horse. She fell off and was hurt. A nurse fixed her arm. Father and daughter then went to the park store and bought some popcorn. She was thirsty, so she had an orange drink.

When they got home, Mother had a birthday party for her. It was a wonderful birthday!

Page 313

Automatic fill in.

Page 314

are not — aren't
you will — you'll
they are — they're
I have — I've
can not — can't
he is — he's
could not — couldn't
I will — I'll
we have — we've
is not — isn't
did not — didn't
they will — they'll
we are — we're

Page 315

football
lighthouse
rainbow
fireman
doorbell
pancake
starfish
cowboy
birdhouse
watchdog
stepladder
eardrum
toothbrush

Page 316

Automatic fill in.

Page 317

Automatic fill in.

Page 318

unhappy
unable
unsafe
unkind
uneven
untied
misfit
misplace
misdeal
misfire
miscount
misspell